CW01085021

TEAM LOTUS
IN FORMULA 1™

RAINER W. SCHLEGELMILCH – HARTMUT LEHBRINK

IMPRINT

COPYRIGHT

© 2011 Edel Germany GmbH, Hamburg/Germany
All photographs © Rainer W. Schlegelmilch
(*www.Schlegelmilch.com*)
with the exception of page 15 Collection Maniago
CD ROM contents © Team Lotus

FOREWORD

Tony Fernandes
Emerson Fittipaldi
Peter Warr

TEXT (*English and German*)

Hartmut Lehbrink

ISBN:

978-3-940004-82-6

PROJECT COORDINATION

Astrid Fischer/edel

ADDITIONAL TRANSLATION (*English*)

and **PROOFREADING**

Gareth Davies

TRANSLATION

Jacqueline Marcella Breuer (*French*),
Llúcia Vivero (*Spanish*), Ramona Ali (*Malaysian*),
Team Lotus (*Chinese*)

ART DIRECTION AND DESIGN

Wolfgang Seidl, SEIDLDESIGN

PRODUCED BY

optimal media production GmbH, Röbel/Germany
Printed and manufactured in Germany

earBOOKS is a division of Edel Germany GmbH
For more information about earBOOKS please visit
www.earbooks.net

REVIVAL OF THE MYTH

KEBANGKITAN SEMULA SEBUAH MITOS

NEUSTART FÜR EINEN MYTHOS

"Being true to tradition means to carry on the flame rather than the ashes", as the French politician and historian Jean Jaurès said.

The fire was once ignited and kept ablaze by the late, great Colin Chapman. It made the Lotus name one of the most resounding in racing, Britain's own Ferrari, as *Motor Sport* recently claimed. 79 grand prix wins, seven constructors' and six drivers' championships speak for themselves, embedded in a wealth of magic and the engineering brilliance of the Norfolk marque.

Chapman's son Clive and his Classic Team Lotus have stoked the glowing embers, keeping the father's heritage alive. And they have done much more than that, impressively documented by the Lotus Festival at Snetterton in June 2010.

It was the enthusiastic Malaysian entrepreneur Tony Fernandes, however, who rekindled the flame. That the Lotus name is back on the grand prix circuits has certainly been one of the best pieces of news for the 2010 season.

"I will do you proud," Tony promised an appreciative and sympathetic crowd at Snetterton. One need not doubt it.

This book pays homage to the three of them.

"Mengekalkan tradisi ertinya terus membawa obor dan bukan sekadar abunya sahaja", kata ahli politik dan ahli sejarah Perancis, Jean Jaurès.

Api obor ini pernah dinyalakan dan dipelihara oleh mendiang Colin Chapman yang agung. Api ini telah menjadikan Lotus salah suatu nama yang paling disebut-sebut di dalam dunia perlumbaan, iaitu Ferrari milik Britain sendiri, sebagaimana yang digambarkan oleh *Motor Sport* baru-baru ini. 79 kejuaraan Grand Prix, tujuh kejohanan pembina dan enam kejohanan pemandu, dikelilingi aneka keajaiban, menjadi bukti kehandalannya dan kehebatan kejuruteraan jenama Norfolk ini.

Anak lelaki Chapman, Clive dan Classic Team Lotus miliknya telah membawa obor ini dan mengabadikan warisan bapanya. Dan mereka telah melakukan jauh lebih banyak daripada itu, didokumenkan oleh Pesta Lotus di Snetterton pada bulan Jun 2010 yang lepas.

Walau bagaimanapun, usahawan agung, Tony Fernandes dari Malaysia, telah menghidupkan semula api ini. Nama Lotus muncul kembali di litar Grand Prix dan sememangnya merupakan antara berita yang terbaik pada musim 2010 ini.

"Saya akan membawa kebanggaan kepada anda," janji Tony kepada khalayak di Snetterton. Tidak diragui bahawa Tony akan mengotakan janjinya itu.

Buku ini memberi penghormatan kepada mereka bertiga.

„Einer Tradition treu zu sein bedeutet, die Flamme weiterzutragen und nicht die Asche", hat der französische Politiker und Historiker Jean Jaurès einmal gesagt.

Colin Chapman hat das Feuer einst entzündet. Er machte Lotus zu einer der ersten Adressen im Rennsport, Englands Ferrari, wie die angesehene Fachpublikation *Motor Sport* es kürzlich ausdrückte. 79 Grand-Prix-Siege, sieben Konstrukteurs- und sechs Fahrerweltmeisterschaften, eingebettet in schiere Magie, sprechen für sich selbst und die technische Brillanz der Marke aus Norfolk.

Chapmans Sohn Clive und sein Classic Team Lotus haben dafür gesorgt, dass die Glut nie erlosch, und zugleich das Erbe seines Vaters am Leben gehalten. Das war Leistung aus Leidenschaft, eindrucksvoll dokumentiert durch das Lotus Festival in Snetterton im Juni 2010.

Der malaysische Unternehmer und Enthusiast Tony Fernandes aber hat das Feuer wieder entfacht. Dass Lotus erneut auf den Grand-Prix-Pisten zu finden ist, gehört zu den guten Nachrichten der aktuellen Saison.

„Ich werde euch stolz machen", versprach Fernandes einer andächtigen und sichtlich bewegten Zuhörerschaft in Snetterton. Man zweifelt nicht daran.

Dieses Buch ist eine Huldigung für alle drei.

EL NUEVO COMIENZO DE UN MITO

«Mantenerse fiel a una tradición significa entregar la llama, no las cenizas», dijo el político e historiador francés Jean Jaurès.

Colin Chapman encendió el fuego una vez: convirtió a Lotus en uno de los grandes de las carreras, el Ferrari de Inglaterra, como lo denominó hace poco *MotorSport*, publicación alemana del sector. 79 Grandes Premios, siete Campeonatos Mundiales de Constructores y seis de Pilotos, intercalados con magia pura, hablan por sí mismos y a favor de la brillantez técnica de la marca de Norfolk.

El hijo de Chapman, Clive, y su Classic Team Lotus se han ocupado de que la llama no se apague, manteniendo a la vez la herencia del padre viva. Los logros conseguidos han sido fruto de la pasión, como quedó patente de forma impresionante en el Festival Lotus en Snetterton, en junio de 2010.

El empresario malayo y entusiasta Tony Fernandes ha vuelto a avivar el fuego. De nuevo es posible encontrar a Lotus en las pistas de los Grandes Premios, una de las grandes noticias de la temporada actual.

«Haré que estéis orgullosos», prometió Fernandes a un público entregado y visiblemente emocionado en Snetterton. Nadie lo duda.

Este libro es un homenaje a los tres.

序言: 傳奇再現

如法國政治家及歷史學家尚. 饒勒斯所言, 維護傳統不是保存灰燼, 而是留住火種。

已故的科林查普曼(Colin Chapman)點燃了蓮花傳奇的火苗, 並讓這個名字持續在賽車界發出耀眼的光芒, 最近更被賽車雜誌Motor Sport譽為英國的法拉利。79場F1大賽優勝、7次構造車商世界冠軍及6次車手總冠軍的光輝紀錄, 已足以替這個擁有神奇力量和工程智慧的諾福克跑車品牌說明一切。

查普曼的兒子克里夫(Clive)和他的經典蓮花車隊(Classic Team Lotus)為這團灼熱的火繼續添加燃料, 將其父親留下的傳統發揚光大。他們做的當然不只這些, 所有的事蹟都在2010年6月於斯內特頓(Snetterton)舉辦的蓮花慶祝活動(Lotus Festival)中詳細的呈現出來。

而讓這團火燃燒的更炙熱的是來自馬來西亞的熱情企業家東尼費南達斯(Tony Fernandes)。他讓蓮花的名字重新回到F1大賽的賽道, 這肯定是2010年賽季最重要的新聞之一。

東尼在斯內特頓向一群熱情的支持群眾承諾「我將讓你們以我為傲」。而這將是不容置疑的事實。

在此藉本書向上述三位表達敬意。

RENAISSANCE D'UN MYTHE

Selon Jean Jaurès, politicien et historien français, « être fidèle à la tradition, c'est être fidèle à la flamme et non à la cendre ».

A l'époque Colin Chapman fit naitre la flamme. Lotus devenait une adresse que l'on se passe en douce dans le sport automobile, la Ferrari anglaise, comme l'a récemment surnommé la revue spécialisée *Motor Sport*. 79 victoires GP, sept titres de champion du monde des constructeurs et six titres pilotes sous l'effet d'un « souffle magique » plaident en faveur du brio technique de la marque issue du Norfolk.

Son fils Clive et le Classic Team Lotus ont conservé la flamme et assuré la pérennité du patrimoine de son père. Cette passion de la performance fut documentée par le Lotus Festival ayant eu lieu sur le circuit de Snetterton en juin 2010.

L'entrepreneur malais et enthousiaste Tony Fernandes fit renaître la flamme. Les retrouvailles avec Lotus sur les circuits GP est une des meilleures notices de la saison actuelle.

La promesse personnelle de Fernandes donnée à l'auditoire visiblement ému à Snetterton, « Je vous rendrais fier ». Personne ne s'en doute.

Ce livre est en hommage à tous les trois.

EMERSON FITTIPALDI

I'm very happy to write the foreword for this beautiful book about the history of Lotus in motor racing. It is a deserved tribute to an icon of British racing heritage. Writing about Lotus for me is, in many ways, like writing about my alma mater. It is with Team Lotus that I had many of my first victories in Formula 3, Formula 2, and then Formula 1, and of course it is with the beloved Lotus 72 ("John Player Special") that I won my first world championship in 1972.

Of course, much of Lotus' success in motor racing was due to the genius of Colin Chapman, who was a mentor for so many great champions like Jim Clark, Graham Hill, Jochen Rindt, and Mario Andretti. Colin's concept of designing and building lighter cars, employing aerodynamics and other concepts derived from aeronautical engineering, and his never ending quest for new ideas and inventions was responsible for much of the evolution of the Formula 1 racing car from the sixties to the eighties. And we cannot forget that he was the first in Formula 1 to look for sponsors and have their logos on his cars, something which today we take for granted, but was an absolute novelty back then.

My history with the make started in 1969, when I was invited to race in Formula 3 with a Lotus car, part of the Lotus Components Team. With this car I won the British F3 Championship in 69 and then went on to race in Formula 2, finally being invited to join the Formula 1 team in 1970. Joining the team that was fighting for the championship with Jochen Rindt as the main driver was something which I could only have dreamed of just a couple of years before.

In my time, the team revolved around Colin and his restless quest to make his cars better and quicker. I learned very much from Colin, and owe to him much of my development as a driver and my victories in the early seventies. We had a very close rapport, where he'd closely listen to my comments about how the car was handling and knew exactly what needed to be changed to improve the car for the next session.

To this day, I have great pleasure in driving the Lotus 72 at events throughout the world. Forty years later it's still a fantastic car in terms of handling, and this is something which cannot be said of all racing cars of that era.

Because of so many innovations and victories Lotus has a very special place in the history of motor racing, and this book brilliantly illustrates the fact with fantastic photos. Enjoy it as much as I do!

Emerson Fittipaldi

TONY FERNANDES

"Pride and Responsibility". These are the two words which strike me as being the most poignant when I consider the challenge of bringing the Lotus name back into Formula 1. It was on September 12th 2009 that we finally gained our entry to the 2010 world championship, leaving us very little time to build a competitive and reliable car. So, just over a year ago, together with my Deputy Team Principals, SM Nasarudin and Kamarudin Meranun, we began work on what is the next chapter of the Team Lotus Formula 1 story.

We were all immensely proud to have had the support of Clive and Hazel Chapman in our first year and it was at the 2010 British GP in Silverstone that Hazel officially opened our new motorhome, and I feel greatly honoured to have had their blessing and encouragement as we set out to build on the legacy of Team Lotus in Formula 1. I am also very proud of my whole team – from Mike Gascoyne, our talented Chief Technical Officer – to every single team member who has helped to build Team Lotus in such a short space of time.

With pride also comes the responsibility of achieving success. My personal mantra is "keep dreaming, believe in yourself, and never take no for an answer" and I feel that, with this attitude, we will overcome the many challenges that face us as we strive to make Team Lotus a success.

Finally, I would like to thank Rainer and Hartmut – for all of your support so far and in sharing the belief that we will once again see a Team Lotus driver on the top step of the podium. I started this journey with a clear vision and goal, and with you as part of our extended team, we have the drive and passion to see our green and yellow cars once again take the chequered flag as winners.

Tony Fernandes

PETER WARR

It is absolutely no surprise that so many years after the squad stopped racing Team Lotus remains one of the iconic names in the history of motor sport. From the plain British racing green with pinstripes in yellow matching the yellow wheels, to the broad central yellow stripe over the green of the Jim Clark era, to the red and gold of the Graham Hill and Jochen Rindt era, to the black and gold of the Emerson Fittipaldi, Ronnie Peterson, Mario Andretti and Ayrton Senna years the team is held in the highest esteem and still has a fan base that is probably second only to that of Ferrari.

Team Lotus was very special primarily due to the all-pervading influence of its founder, the late Colin Chapman. As all of the exceptional abilities with which he was endowed were able to be expressed in the form and deeds of a racing team Team Lotus never lacked design genius, engineering talent, innovative thinking, competitive spirit and a team of very highly motivated individuals. Colin was brilliant at them all.

Bring all these together and mix in Colin's absolute refusal to believe that anything was impossible, that there was no job that could not be finished before the next race and an ever present willingness to take performance to the limit and the ingredients were present not only to succeed but also to engender an heroic following for the most successful racing team of the period. It won more championships, races and claimed more pole positions than any other team in the same years.

Readers should be reminded that not only did Team Lotus win 79 grands prix and set over 100 pole positions while taking seven world championships but it competed and won at Indianapolis and in Indycars, the Tasman Series, Formula Two, Formula Three, Sports Racing Cars, GT and the Formula Libre categories.

Many of these wins added up to further championships in the various classes of racing. Numerous wins were also gained in non-championship Formula 1 events.

Team Lotus was never endowed with award winning factories or extensive capital assets. It was the people who worked in the team and the expertise, hard work, endurance and competitive spirit of that fantastic bunch of colleagues which gave Team Lotus its special cachet. It is interesting to see that, hard training school that it undoubtedly was, there is hardly an organization in motor racing still today that does not include an ex-Team Lotus member of staff and usually one in a senior and responsible position so valued are they. We worked hard (usually the last team to leave the garages at night), we played hard, enjoyed great success and had to endure some of the most bitter moments in motor sport of all time.

After the very premature death of Colin Chapman, those of us who remained endeavoured to retain all the traditions, standards, attitudes and outlook that had made the team what it had been. It is pleasing to note that to a great extent we succeeded, with grand prix wins continuing until 1987.

It is a source of immense pride to have been part of the story and a delight that the name is to return to Formula 1.

Peter Warr
*France 2010**

On 4 October 2010 Peter Warr died of a heart attack in his home in South France.

TABLE OF
CONTENTS

1987–1990

1991–1994

2010

CHANGE OF
COLOURS:
CAMEL

96

LAST
BASTION:
HITACHI

104

COMING
FULL CIRCLE:
LOTUS RACING

116

WINNERS:
**EIGHT LOTUS
DRIVERS**

134

PACESETTERS:
**FOUR LOTUS
GRAND PRIX CARS**

152

HELMSMEN:
**TWO LOTUS
LEADERS**

158

**APPENDIX
CD ROM CONTENT
BIBLIOGRAPHY**

164

1

TEAM LOTUS

FIRST FLUSH:
TEAM LOTUS

THE FIRST TEN YEARS OF TEAM LOTUS IN BRITISH RACING GREEN WERE A PERIOD OF TRIUMPH AND TRIBULATIONS. THEY BROUGHT TWO F1 CONSTRUCTORS' TITLES FOR LOTUS AND TWO DRIVERS' TITLES FOR JIM CLARK IN 1963 AND '65, BUT ALSO THE DEATHS OF THE GREAT SCOT HIMSELF, MIKE SPENCE AND ALAN STACEY AT THE WHEEL OF LOTUS RACING CARS.

1958-1968

YEAR	CARS	DRIVERS	GP VICTORIES
1958	Lotus 12-Climax 4 Lotus 16-Climax 4	Cliff Allison / Graham Hill / Alan Stacey	—
1959	Lotus 16-Climax 4	Cliff Allison / Graham Hill / Alan Stacey	—
1960	Lotus 18-Climax 4	Stirling Moss (Rob Walker), Innes Ireland / John Surtees / Jim Clark / David Piper	MON (Moss) / USA (Moss)
1961	Lotus 21-Climax 4 Lotus 18/21-Climax 4 (Rob Walker)	Stirling Moss (Rob Walker) / Innes Ireland / Jim Clark	MON (Moss) / GER (Moss) / USA (Ireland)
1962	Lotus 25-Climax V8 Lotus 18/21-Climax 4 (Rob Walker)	Jim Clark / Trevor Taylor / Peter Arundell (works) Stirling Moss / Maurice Trintignant (Walker), Innes Ireland / Masten Gregory (UDT Laystall)	BEL / GB / USA (all Clark)
1963	Lotus 25-Climax V8	Jim Clark / Trevor Taylor	BEL / HOL / FRA / GB / ITA / MEX / SA (all Clark)
1964	Lotus 25-Climax V8 Lotus 33-Climax V8	Jim Clark / Peter Arundell / Mike Spence	HOL / BEL / GB (all Clark)
1965	Lotus 33-Climax V8	Jim Clark / Mike Spence	SA / BEL / FRA / GB / HOL / GER (all Clark)
1966	Lotus 33-Climax V8 Lotus 43-BRM H16	Jim Clark / Mike Spence / Peter Arundell	USA (Clark)
1967	Lotus 33-Climax V8 Lotus 43-BRM H16 Lotus 49-Cosworth V8	Jim Clark / Graham Hil	HOL / GB / USA / MEX (all Clark)
1968	Lotus 49-Cosworth V8	Jim Clark / Graham Hill	SA (Clark) / end of British racing green era, Clark's last GP

01 First ever GP for Lotus: Graham Hill at Monaco in 1958, in a type 12-Climax

02 Graham Hill, Lotus 16-Climax, 1958 – still front-engined

03 Stirling Moss, winner of the 1960 Monaco GP, Lotus 18-Climax. The car belongs to private entrant Rob Walker.

04 Graham Hill, Lotus 16-Climax, leading Carroll Shelby, Aston Martin DBR4, Zandvoort, 1959

05 GP debut of the Lotus 18-Climax: Innes Ireland at Buenos Aires, 1960. Ireland went on to finish sixth.

The origins were humble indeed. But already from an early age, it became obvious that Colin Chapman had a penchant for machinery that was fast both on land and in the air. While studying mechanical engineering at University College, London, he flew solo for the first time in 1947 in the renowned academy's Air Squadron. A year later he did his National Service as a Royal Air Force pilot. As soon as he was discharged from the RAF, he began building his own cars under the Lotus name at Hornsey, North London, and racing them. On 1 January 1952, with a generous £25 loan from his girlfriend and future wife Hazel Williams in his pocket, Chapman established Lotus Engineering Ltd, based in a stable behind his parents' Railway Hotel, still at Hornsey.

01 Jim Clark at the wheel of the tiny Lotus 23 was the sensation of the Nürburgring 1000 km race on 27 May 1962.

02 Bespectacled American Masten Gregory, Lotus 24-BRM, alongside Innes Ireland, Lotus 24-Climax, at Monza, 1962

03 Jack Brabham, Spa-Francorchamps, Lotus 24-Climax, 1962. The car would later belong to German gentleman racer Dieter Streve-Mülhens.

04 Jim Clark rushes up the *Eau Rouge* right-hander at Spa, Lotus 25-Climax, 1962.

05 Start of the 1962 Belgian GP, Graham Hill in the BRM P57, Innes Ireland, Lotus 24-Climax (UDT Laystall Racing Team), in the background

After rapid success with the 1953 Mk VI and the streamlined 1954 Mk VIII sports car, Team Lotus split off from the small parent company in 1954. They had entered the British national stage with a bang but, after a fourth place for a Mk VIII at the 1954 Eifelrennen, the Lotus logo also began to make an indelible impression overseas.

Chapman quickly made a name for himself squeezing crucial fractions of time out of his machines by means of exploiting regulation loopholes. He was still an ambitious racing driver, too, winning an F2 event at Brands Hatch in his Lotus 11 in 1956, while the following year Cliff Allison set a new lap record aboard the F2 Lotus 12 in the prestigious International Trophy race at Silverstone. At the same time, Chapman

occasionally lent a helping hand to improve other people's cars. He designed, for instance, a light spaceframe for Tony Vandervell's F1 Vanwalls in 1956 and upgraded the suspension of Raymond Mays' BRM grand prix vehicles in 1957.

He also joined the Vanwall team for the 1956 French Grand Prix at Reims. Chapman was to race a third entry for the outfit alongside Mike Hawthorn and Harry Schell, but he locked a brake in practice at the *Thillois* hairpin whilst battling with his compatriot Hawthorn. The two cars collided, denting Colin's ego and pulling the plug on what might have resulted in a burgeoning Formula 1 career for Chapman. In all probability, as jazzband leader, hobby racer and Chapman chum Chris Barber

remembers, his retirement from active sport was triggered by the customary end-of-season event at Brands Hatch on 26 December 1958, after dicing with rising star Jim Clark in works Lotus Elites. His true vocation, he suddenly realized, was conceiving and building racing cars.

With the Coventry Climax more competitive thanks to their two-litre FPF engines (a 2.5-litre version exploiting the current Formula 1 regulations to the full was to follow in 1959), Chapman decided to enter grand prix racing in 1958. He fielded a pair of Lotus 12s for Graham Hill and Allison in that season's second race at Monaco. Hill lost a wheel, as he would on a number of occasions later on, whilst Allison took the chequered flag a demoralizing 13 laps behind the winner Maurice Trintignant

in a Cooper-Climax. However, he finished fourth in the Belgian GP a month later, earning his three points in the final standings. Chapman's cars were still front-engined, unlike the all-conquering Coopers in the next two seasons, so they stood little chance against their established competitors.

But that changed dramatically after the Lotus supremo had introduced the elegant little mid-engined Type 18 which swept the board in Formula Junior racing in 1960. In the meantime, Lotus had moved to a bigger factory in Cheshunt, Hertfordshire, a part of the Greater London Urban Area. Expansion had been inevitable to produce the Elite road car, which had been an instant sales success.

01 Jo Siffert, Lotus 21-Climax (Ecurie Filipinetti), Spa-Francorchamps, 1962. It was the first GP for the Swiss.

02 A thoughtful Jim Clark on the Monza pit wall in 1962. In the race, his Lotus 25-Climax will retire with transmission trouble.

01 Jim Clark, Lotus 25-Climax, and
   Graham Hill, BRM P57, approaching
   Gasometer, Monaco, 1963

02 Jim Clark spinning his Lotus round
   the *Gasometer* bend, Monaco, 1963

RIGHT
03 Retirement for the Scot later in the
   race, owing to faulty gear selection,
   despite frantic assistance from
   marshals and officials

In its Formula 1 guise, the Lotus 18 handed Chapman the marque's first GP victory on a silver platter at Monaco, Stirling Moss driving the blue and white private entry of Scottish whisky heir Rob Walker. The balding Londoner was to repeat the feat through the streets of the Principality the following year at the wheel of the same car, beating the new Ferraris against all odds. Apart from another Moss triumph at the Nürburgring and Innes Ireland's first win in a Lotus works car at the finale in Watkins Glen, it had been the shark-nosed red Ferrari 156s which dominated that particular season under the new 1500 cc F1 regulations.

The battle for the 1962 championship between Jim Clark and BRM star Graham Hill was decided in the last round at East London in favour of Hill, after Lotus

01 Start of the 1963 Dutch GP: smoking tyres in the first row, from the cars of pole-sitter and eventual race winner Jim Clark, Lotus 25-Climax, Graham Hill, BRM P57, Bruce McLaren, Cooper T66-Climax

man Clark had been sidelined with an oil leak. The fumes escaping from a broken exhaust had ended his triumphant drive in the tiny twin-cam-engined Lotus 23 sports car with which he had dominated the 1000 km race on a rain-soaked and slippery Nürburgring. In 1963, however, the Scotsman came back with a vengeance when he took the revolutionary Lotus 25 (chassis R4) to an amazing seven victories, securing titles both for himself and for Team Lotus. He also came in runner-up at Indianapolis with the 29.

In 1964 the F1 title fight was again taken down to the very last race at Mexico City, with Clark, Hill and Ferrari driver John Surtees all still in the running. A grand prix full of dramatic incidents saw the former motorcycle champion emerge as the winner of that year's championship by the narrowest of margins, his car famously painted in the blue and white colours of the North American Racing Team. In contrast, the 1965 season turned out to be the most fertile and rewarding for Lotus so far. Favourite son Jimmy Clark gave the Cheshunt squad six victories in the 33, securing their second drivers' and constructors' crowns. He also won the Tasman Series and, on 31 May, after opting to miss the Monaco Grand Prix, the Indianapolis 500 in the Type 38. His Lotus had been designed and built specifically to drive into the winners' circle in that celebrated blue-

02 Same situation at the 1963 French GP at Reims, with the usual suspects Clark and Hill, this time joined by Dan Gurney, Brabham BT7-Climax

03 Pole position, fastest lap and victory for Clark, French GP, 1963

04 Sharing the same view: Lotus team boss Colin Chapman and driver Jim Clark

01 Season-opener at Monaco 1964, but again no victory in the Principality, Jim Clark, Lotus 25-Climax

02 Brilliant win for Jim Clark – his third at Spa – and the Lotus 25. A victory on the undulating and ultra-fast Ardennes circuit makes up for a lot of Monaco frustration.

riband event. The year was rounded off by the marque dominating the British and French Formula 2 championships with their nimble, multi-purpose 35 chassis.

1966 came as a counterpoint, with the marque somehow caught unprepared by the new three-litre regulations. Until the Italian GP, leading driver Clark could only soldier on with an uncompetitive two-litre Coventry Climax in the rear of his ageing Type 33, plagued by all sorts of troubles. But he did win the US Grand Prix at Watkins Glen in October, his Lotus 43 powered by the complex, overweight and usually unreliable BRM H16 unit. Anticipating later practice, this engine formed part of the car's rear structure. At the same time, Lotus was preparing to be relocated in a new factory on a former USAF airfield at Hethel, Norfolk. The move was completed the following year.

As early as 1966, Colin Chapman had persuaded Ford to invest £100,000 in a new, compact grand prix engine built by Cosworth. In 1967 the pact came spectacularly to fruition. From its first outing in the season's third race at Zandvoort, the Ford V8 had the edge on its competitors, as the Lotus drivers, Jim Clark and Graham Hill, in their DFV-equipped 49s, dominated the Dutch event in terms of sheer speed. But thanks to numerous failures of the green and yellow Hethel cars, it was New Zealander Denny Hulme and the plain, but reliable Brabham-Repco that secured the two championships.

Lotus had meanwhile grown into a flourishing enterprise, selling both racing and road cars such as the Elite, the Elan and the Europa. In 1968, Colin Chapman became a

01 Jump over the hill for Clark and his Lotus 25-Climax at the 1964 Monaco GP, with the Hotel de Paris as an attractive backdrop

02 Jim Clark side by side with his perennial rival Graham Hill, preparing for the Dutch GP amidst the Zandvoort dunes

03 Clark, Lotus 25-Climax, leading Graham Hill, BRM P261 and Dan Gurney, Brabham BT7-Climax, approaches Zandvoort's *Hunzerug* left-hander on the first lap of the 1964 Dutch GP.

04 Jim Clark, Lotus 25-Climax, Monaco 1964. The Station Hairpin is later to morph into Loew's and Hotel Hairpin.

NEXT PAGE

01 Racing is life, the time in between is waiting, says Steve McQueen in his famous *Le Mans* film. This is indeed so – as demonstrated here by Colin Chapman and team-mates Clark and Mike Spence at Clermont-Ferrand, 1965.

02 Duel of the Scots: Slipstreaming battle between pole-man Jim Clark, Lotus 33-Climax (No. 24), and eventual winner Jackie Stewart, BRM P261, at Monza in 1965

01 Fourth and final win at Spa for Jim Clark, Lotus 33-Climax, in atrocious weather conditions, 1965. The appropriately named corner, like *Eau Rouge* just down the hill, is *La Source*.

02 Brickyard triumph: Jim Clark, victor at Indianapolis in 1965, driving the Lotus 38-Ford. The car never ran again until 2010.

03 Lotus supremo Colin Chapman and mechanic Jim Endruweit congratulate Jim Clark on his 1965 victory at the German GP, Clark's only win at the Nürburgring.

NEXT PAGE

01 Thunder, lightning and packed grandstands, as the eventual winner of the 1966 Italian GP, Ludovico Scarfiotti, Ferrari 312/66, powers away from the chequered line, leading Jim Clark, Lotus 43-BRM H16, and his own team-mate and pole-sitter Mike Parkes

millionaire at the tender age of 40, when 48 per cent of his firm was floated on the stock exchange. What was to be expected at the end of the 1967 Formula 1 season materialized at the very beginning of the 1968 motor racing year. The South African Grand Prix at Kyalami on 1 January held in store a resounding Lotus one-two for Clark and Hill. That illustrious driver pairing plus the 49 and its derivatives and successors seemed set to reign supreme for a long time. But Kyalami had been the great Scot's last win. His death in a Formula 2 race at Hockenheim on 7 April 1968 severely and lastingly shook the foundations of the Lotus world. Colin Chapman was devastated.

01 2 pm local time at the Nürburgring. Round six of the 1966 F1 season is about to get going. John Surtees' Cooper T81-Maserati, Jackie Stewart's BRM P261 and Ludovico Scarfiotti's Ferrari Dino 246 have joined Jim Clark's Lotus 33 on the first row of the grid.

02 Jim Clark in the pits, chatting with team-mate Peter Arundell. There is no hurry.

03 Master at work, Clark this time circling his neat Lotus 33 through the *Tarzan* bend in Holland

NEXT PAGE

01 Odd two-seater: Graham Hill gives Jo Siffert a lift during practice at the 1967 Monaco GP.

02 Fisheye view: Jim Clark in the pits during the same event

01 The cars lining up for the 1967 British GP at Silverstone. The final formation is still in the making, so pole-man and eventual winner Jim Clark finds himself next to the Brabham-Repco of Guy Ligier who qualified 21st and last.

02 Sunny break at the 1967 French GP at Le Mans, enjoyed by Clark, Hill and Keith Duckworth

03 The two drivers in professional clothing this time, speaking to influential Ford PR executive Walter Hayes

04 The focus of attention: The new and ready-to-race Cosworth DFV V8 in the rear of the Lotus 49 at Zandvoort in 1967. The engine's creator Keith Duckworth, Lotus boss Colin Chapman and the two drivers marvel at the achievement.

05 While Clark walks to his pit, Keith Duckworth gives his masterpiece, the Cosworth DFV V8, a final check.

06 Clark has won the 1967 British GP in the all-conquering Lotus 49-Cosworth. The mechanics proudly display the trophy after the Scot's 22nd victory for the team.

07 Portrait of two winners: Jim Clark and the Lotus 49, a slender projectile

2

....

GOLD LEAF

GOLD LEAF

BREAKING NEW GROUND AGAIN:
GOLD LEAF TEAM LOTUS

AS THE COST OF RUNNING A GRAND PRIX TEAM ESCALATED
RAPIDLY, FOLLOWING THE INTRODUCTION OF THE THREE-LITRE
FORMULA IN 1966, COLIN CHAPMAN RESORTED TO TAPPING
FINANCIAL RESOURCES BEYOND THE RACING REALM. FROM
1968, HIS CARS APPEARED IN GOLD LEAF COLOURS, WINNING
THE 1968 AND THE 1970 TITLES.

1968-1971

YEAR	CARS	DRIVERS	GP VICTORIES
1968	Lotus 49-Cosworth V8 49B-Cosworth V8	Jim Clark / Graham Hill / Jackie Oliver (works) Jo Siffert (Rob Walker)	ESP (Hill) / MON (Hill) / GB (Siffert) / MEX (Hill)
1969	Lotus 49B-Cosworth V8	Graham Hill / Jochen Rindt / Mario Andretti / John Miles / Richard Attwood (works) / Jo Siffert (Rob Walker)	MON (Hill) / USA (Rindt)
1970	Lotus 49C-Cosworth V8 Lotus 72-Cosworth V8	Jochen Rindt / John Miles / Emerson Fittipaldi / Reine Wisell (works) Graham Hill (Rob Walker)	MON (Rindt) / HOL (Rindt) / FRA (Rindt) GB (Rindt) / GER (Rindt) / USA (Fittipaldi)
1971	Lotus 72C-Cosworth V8 Lotus 72D-Cosworth V8 Turbine Lotus 56B-Pratt & Whitney	Emerson Fittipaldi / Reine Wisell	—

Towards the end of the sixties, the cost of grand prix racing was soaring. At the same time, TV began to be a major factor in GP coverage and the sport's governing body, the FIA, changed the regulations to permit messages of non-trade sponsors being carried by the cars.

Colin Chapman seized the opportunity, pointing out that as man was about to set out for the moon, Formula 1 needed more complex and sophisticated machinery to comply with an age of advanced technology. Needless to say, this would prove more costly. External sources of revenue had to be found to bridge the gap in funding effectively.

The notion went down well with cigarette manufacturer John Player. On 20 January 1968 Jim Clark won the Lady Wigram Trophy race, a Tasman round at Christchurch, New Zealand, in a Lotus 49T bearing the red, white and gold livery of the Player's brand Gold Leaf. It met with a controversial reception, to say the least, as purists slammed Lotus for abusing their cars as mobile advertisements. On 17 March the new colour scheme made its European debut in the Race of Champions at Brands Hatch, and it was also seen on the poor remains of Clark's Type 48 Formula 2 wreckage at Hockenheim on 7 April. Its grand prix premiere took place at Jarama on 12 May, the colourful 49 again in the hands of Hill, who went on to win that year's world championship with another two victories, as well as securing the constructors' crown for GLTL.

01 As John Surtees in the Honda RA301 hurtles past, Jo Siffert in Rob Walker's Lotus 49 has just stopped to borrow a dry visor from works driver Graham Hill. The Londoner retired from the 1968 French GP at Rouen with drive shaft failure on his Type 49B-Cosworth.

02 Still life at Spa-Francorchamps, with Lotus 49B, black and white helmet, gloves and Graham Hill in front of the pits

01 At the German Grand Prix, Jochen Rindt saves the tyres of his Lotus 49B-Cosworth for a tiny moment.

In 1969 Hill notched up his customary first place in Monaco, which ultimately proved to be his final grand prix triumph. The team's other win, at Watkins Glen, was secured courtesy of new Lotus recruit Jochen Rindt. During the Spanish GP at Montjuich Park, the pair shared a ghastly experience due to the failure of their 49Bs' huge but fragile rear wings. Within eleven laps they collapsed, first on Hill's and then on Rindt's car. The Austrian speared into the Englishman's abandoned vehicle and overturned. As a consequence, the swaying devices were banned after the first day of practice of the following GP at Monaco, later to be replaced by less spectacular, but more solid constructions.

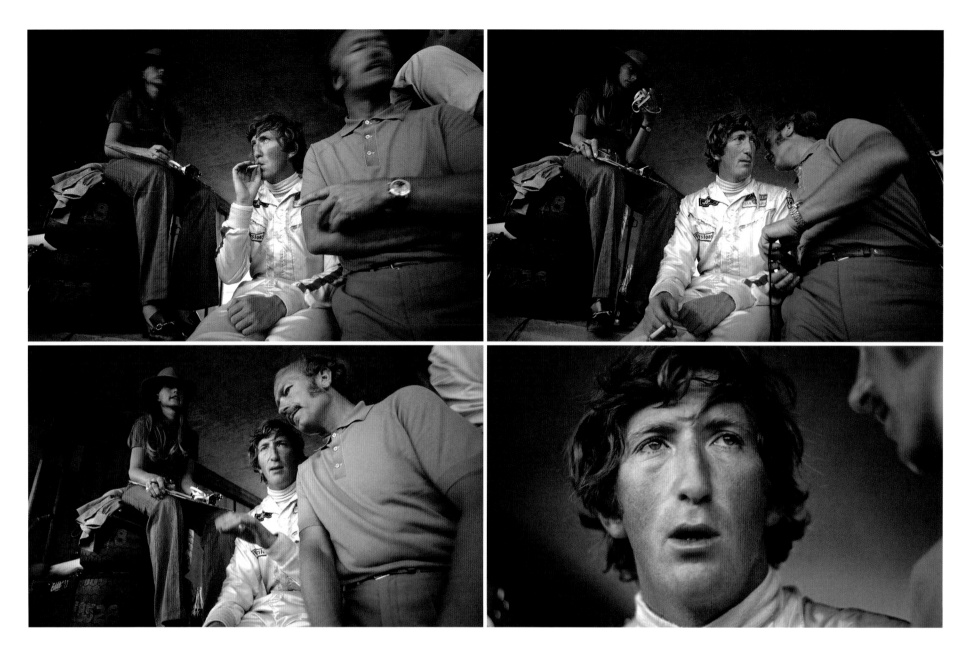

01 Austrian Rindt, with his time-keeping wife Nina and Lotus head Colin Chapman, during his home grand prix weekend at the majestic Österreichring, 1970 – his last race

02 Informal meeting of Lotus men Emerson Fittipaldi, Colin Chapman, John Miles and Jochen Rindt at Hockenheim. Rindt would beat Ferrari driver Jacky Ickx by a whisker.

03 Winner of the 1970 German GP, Jochen Rindt, Lotus 72-Cosworth. It was to be the popular Austrian's last victory.

01 Graham Hill, Lotus 49C-Cosworth (Rob Walker, with sponsorship from the Brooke Bond Oxo tea company), Hockenheim, 1970, retirement

02 Graham Hill, Lotus 49C-Cosworth, Clermont-Ferrand, 1970, 10th

03 Graham Hill, Lotus 49C-Cosworth, Monaco, 1970, 5th

04 Approaching *Tobacconist's Corner* at Monaco, ultimate race winner Jochen Rindt in the Lotus 49C-Cosworth leads Piers Courage, de Tomaso 505, Jo Siffert, March 701 and Bruce McLaren, McLaren M14A, all Cosworth-engined. Three of these men would not survive the motor racing year 1970, while Siffert would be killed at Brands Hatch in 1971.

The former bomber airfield at Hethel and its runways morphed into a makeshift testing facility, while more serious tests were conducted at the nearby Snetterton circuit. Offices and design studios were based at Ketteringham Hall, which became the garrison of both Team Lotus and Lotus Cars, from 1969 on, together with Lotus Components, under the banner of the Group Lotus holding company. The 1970 Spanish GP saw the first appearance of the radical wedge-shaped Type 72, featuring hip-mounted radiators, innovative torsion-bar suspension and a multi-element overhanging rear wing. Continual problems with the suspension in particular saw Lotus revert to the proven 49s at Monaco. Rindt carried the day after Jack Brabham slid into the straw bales in the last corner.

01–03 Star in the making: Emerson Fittipaldi in 1971 at Monaco, his eighth grand prix for the Lotus marque.
Rolf Stommelen in his Surtees TS9-Cosworth passes in the wet.

The Austrian went on to notch up another four victories with the new car before his fatal accident at Monza, adding to grand prix history the dubious dignity of being a posthumous world champion, since his tally could not be surpassed in the remaining four rounds.

After eleven more or less successful seasons, Lotus finished 1971 without a single win, the year overshadowed by Rindt's untimely death. But the team also frittered away energy experimenting with the gas-turbine-powered 56B and the Type 63, mistakenly believed to herald a future in which the ever-increasing power of grand prix cars had to be conveyed to the tarmac via their four wheels. The 72 and its various

derivatives struggled, however, with their new low-profile Firestone tyres, though the removal of anti-squat and anti-dive from its suspension greatly enhanced the model's roadholding.

Colin Chapman had already proved his versatility in various other fields. He further extended the range of his activities when he acquired Moonraker Boats. Nobody was surprised when he immediately made his presence felt, making drastic changes in design and manufacturing.

01 At the British GP Swedish Lotus recruit Reine Wisell spends 90 unhappy minutes at the wheel of the Lotus 56B turbine car, his progress further hampered by a throttle that does not open fully.

02 Wisell's Lotus 56B-Pratt & Whitney under scrutiny from Colin Chapman in the Silverstone pit lane, with Emerson Fittipaldi looking on

03 At Monza, it is the Brazilian's turn to drive the whishing exotic. The legal ramifications of the Rindt tragedy in the preceding year precluded GLTL from appearing in their own guise. So the car is painted in black and gold livery and entered by the Bahamas-based Worldwide Racing concern, which in the past looked after the Indy vehicles of the make. Although expected to do well at this circuit, it plays no part in the sensational finish of the 1971 Italian GP.

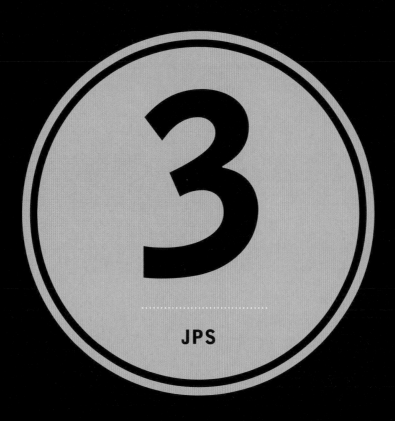

3
JPS

PREVAILINGLY BLACK AND GOLD:
JOHN PLAYER SPECIAL

1972 SAW THE BEGINNING OF A LASTING PARTNERSHIP WITH
CIGARETTE BRAND JOHN PLAYER, IN WHOSE BLACK AND GOLD
COLOURS THE TEAM WON TWO DRIVERS' TITLES FOR EMERSON
FITTIPALDI IN 1972 AND MARIO ANDRETTI IN 1978, AS WELL AS
THREE CONSTRUCTORS' CROWNS IN 1972, 1973 AND 1978.

1972-1986

YEAR	CARS	DRIVERS	GP VICTORIES
1972	Lotus 72D-Cosworth V8	Emerson Fittipaldi / Reine Wisell / Dave Walker	ESP / BEL / GB / AUT / ITA (all Fittipaldi)
1973	Lotus 72D and E-Cosworth V8	Emerson Fittipaldi / Ronnie Peterson	ARG (Fittipaldi) / BRA (Fittipaldi) / ESP (Fittipaldi)
			FRA (Peterson) / AUT (Peterson) / ITA (Peterson) / USA (Peterson)
1974	Lotus 72E and 76-Cosworth V8	Ronnie Peterson / Jacky Ickx	MON / FRA / ITA (all Peterson)
1975	Lotus 72E-Cosworth V8	Ronnie Peterson / Jacky Ickx / John Watson / Jim Crawford	—
1976	Lotus 77-Cosworth V8	Mario Andretti / Ronnie Peterson / Gunnar Nilsson	JAP (Andretti)
1977	Lotus 78-Cosworth V8	Mario Andretti / Gunnar Nilsson	USAW (Andretti) / ESP (Andretti) / BEL (Nilsson)
			FRA (Andretti) / ITA (Andretti)
1978	Lotus 78 and 79-Cosworth V8	Mario Andretti / Ronnie Peterson / Jean-Pierre Jarier	ARG (Andretti) / SA (Peterson) / BEL (Andretti) / ESP (Andretti)
			FRA (Andretti) / GER (Andretti) / AUT (Peterson) / HOL (Andretti)
1979	Lotus 79 and 80-Cosworth V8	Mario Andretti / Carlos Reutemann	—
1980	Lotus 81-Cosworth V8	Mario Andretti / Elio de Angelis / Nigel Mansell	—
1981	Lotus 81 and 81B, 87, 88 and 88B-Cosworth V8	Elio de Angelis / Nigel Mansell	—
1982	Lotus 87B and 91-Cosworth V8	Elio de Angelis / Nigel Mansell / Geoff Lees	AUT (de Angelis)
1983	Lotus 92-Cosworth V8 Lotus 93T-Renault V6	Elio de Angelis / Nigel Mansell	—
1984	Lotus 95T-Renault V6	Elio de Angelis / Nigel Mansell	—
1985	Lotus 97T-Renault V6	Elio de Angelis / Ayrton Senna	POR (Senna) / RSM (de Angelis) / BEL (Senna)
1986	Lotus 98T-Renault V6	Ayrton Senna / Johnny Dumfries	ESP / USAE (both Senna)

A new deal was announced in November 1971: From the next season onwards, Lotus Formula 1 cars would sport the black and gold colours of the John Player cigarette brand and be entered as John Player Specials. The joint venture, not least designed to throw down the gauntlet to market rival Marlboro, was ultimately to last for 15 years, sometimes augmented by others, like Olympus in 1978, Essex Oil in 1980 and 1981, DeLonghi in 1986, interrupted just briefly in 1979 when Martini sponsored Lotus for one season.

Colin Chapman had pulled off another coup, going one step further. What Vance Packard had once called "The Hidden Persuaders" were no longer hidden at all. Not only did the advertising medium carry the product's logo and colours (as did

01 During practice for the 1972 French GP at Clermont-Ferrand Emerson Fittipaldi in the 72D-Cosworth was feeling unwell, but in the race no one looked like matching the Brazilian – apart from Tyrrell driver Jackie Stewart, who secured a majestic win that day.

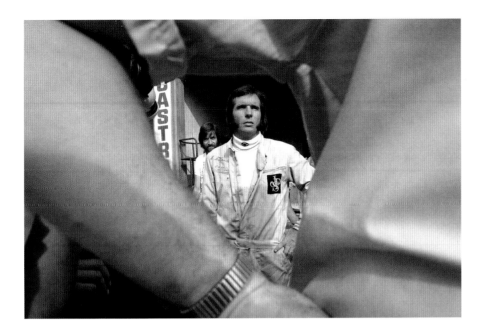

02 A boyish Fittipaldi at Monza, looking amazed. He went on, nevertheless, to clinch his first world championship in the Royal Park, as did Jim Clark in 1963 and Jackie Stewart in 1969.

03 The magnificent Österreichring is the setting for one of the 1972 season's finest grands prix, virtually assuring Fittipaldi of the title. But he has to battle throughout the race before emerging victorious.

04 Keeping a clear view: Fending off the rains in Monaco where, however, BRM driver Pete Gethin reigned supreme on an unforgettably miserable day.

05 Turning the tables on the preceding year's champion Jackie Stewart, Emerson Fittipaldi in the Lotus 72D a.k.a JPS pulls off his third win of the season at Brands Hatch. He had already earned victory there at the Race of Champions in March.

some of the Lotus production cars), it had also become synonymous with the team, anticipating the Red Bulls at the beginning of the next century. From 1976 through to 1979, the current Lotus models were rebranded John Player Specials Mk I to IV.

After the fallow year of 1971 Lotus began to get going again. Fond memories harked back to Emerson Fittipaldi's win at Watkins Glen in 1970, with Lotus novice Reine Wisell third. Like Graham Hill's victory at Jarama shortly after Clark's death in 1968, it had come at a crucial moment, as the team was shaken to the core by Jochen Rindt's Monza tragedy. The young Brazilian won the 1972 world title, becoming the youngest ever F1 champion at the time. The now fully developed 72, he said later, was the best Formula 1 car he had ever driven. It also secured the outfit its third constructors'

championship, followed immediately by the fourth the following season. Meanwhile, Ronnie Peterson had joined Fittipaldi. Very much on a par, and without Chapman dictating any pecking order, the pair took points from one another. They finished second and third in the drivers' standings, permitting Jackie Stewart to win his third crown in a Tyrrell that was rarely a match for the Lotus.

The 72's would-be successor, the 76 launched in 1974, proved to be a disappointment. Convincing in theory, with the same suspension layout and geometry as the 72, but a revised and lighter monocoque as well as a clutch that could be engaged by operating a gear-knob button, it failed completely to live up to expectations. So the revised 72E had to fly the JPS flag again. It was still a winner, the blond Swede scoring three firsts

01 A visit to the pits during practice for the 1973 French GP at Le Castellet. Soon afterwards Fittipaldi will be on his way to third slot on the grid.

02 In the race the Brazilian is sidelined after a collision with Jody Scheckter, the young and wild McLaren driver, at the end of lap 42. But it's "Emmo's" fault.

03 So it is team-mate Ronnie Peterson, seen here during a practice session, who wins his first grand prix by a comfortable margin from Tyrrell star François Cevert.

01 Jacky Ickx, who has joined Lotus at the beginning of the 1974 campaign, relaxes in the pit.

02 The Belgian in full swing at Monaco in the same year. His car is the 72E-Cosworth, the 76 having failed to live up to expectations.

03 Business talk between Peterson and a greying Colin Chapman at Monza

04 Team-mates Jacky Ickx and Ronnie Peterson at Zandvoort. It's not their day, with ninth place for the Belgian and a lowly tenth for "SuperSwede".

01 Ronnie Peterson and the ageing 72E in 1975, slightly airborne in the *Flugplatz* section of the Nürburgring

02 With Colin Chapman every inch the commander, Peterson talks to his mechanic at the Ring. The Swede's technical input was, however, negligible, to say the least.

03 Peterson avoiding contact with the tarmac somewhere in the Eifel mountains

01 Mario Andretti, enjoying the benefit of full employment at Lotus now, in the beautiful but less than efficient Type 77. The year is 1976.

02 Lotus team-mates Mario Andretti and Gunnar Nilsson at Zeltweg, where they are to finish in third (Nilsson) and fifth (Andretti) position

03 Helmeted and ready for action: Mario Andretti and …

04 … Gunnar Nilsson

01 Gunnar Nilsson, Lotus 78-Cosworth, a.k.a JPS Mark III, at speed in 1977, Jarama, Spain

02 The `other´ Swede again, ready to race at Dijon-Prenois, where he passed the chequered flag in fourth position

03 Leading Lauda's Ferrari 312 T2 on the same occasion. Which is also the order in which they crossed the finishing line

04 Home victory for Mario Andretti at Long Beach, his first in the 1977 season

01 Unequal bedfellows: 1978 Lotus team-mates Mario Andretti and Ronnie Peterson

02 The Lotus men's drying overalls at Hockenheim

03 A familiar sight: The start of the German GP at Hockenheim with the two Lotus 79s in the lead, as so often in the 1978 season. Niki Lauda's red and blue Brabham BT46-Alfa Romeo breathes down Andretti's neck.

04 Andretti waiting patiently at Le Castellet, under the watchful eyes of his boss Colin Chapman

05 Mario Andretti, Lotus 78-Cosworth, Monaco, 1978

with it. But then the model, considered a beauty by some and a coffin by others, had shot its bolt. In a repeat of 1971, there were no wins for Lotus in 1975. The black and gold squad plummeted to a humble seventh place in the constructors' standings, with a meagre tally of nine points, unprecedented since 1960. In the mid-seventies the grand prix circuits were Ferrari and McLaren territory, the irony being that Gordon Coppuck's McLaren M23, James Hunt's 1976 world championship car, was strongly inspired by the Lotus 72.

New thinking was urgently called for. During a holiday in 1975, Colin Chapman used the time to readjust mentally to the changed conditions. One step was to persuade Mario Andretti to commit to a full-time F1 programme with Lotus from 1976. Of

course he had not forgotten that the American, paying a flying visit to grand prix racing at the 1968 US GP, had put his 49 on pole position at Watkins Glen. Chapman addressed Andretti at an opportune moment as both were experiencing a critical phase in their careers. Mario agreed, acknowledging that he had always had faith in Chapman and would not leave him in the lurch. Early in 1975, Lotus had put together a new design team, with men like Geoff Aldridge and Martin Ogilvie reporting to Peter Warr. They mapped out the concept of a car with variable wheelbase, track, suspension set-up and weight distribution to adapt to individual circuits – the "adjustable" Lotus 77. It was, however, much simpler when it hit the tracks, and again proved to be only an interim solution. But in the last race of the 1976 season, at a rain-soaked Mount Fuji circuit in Japan, both Andretti and Chapman were back in

04 Essex man and title sponsor David Thieme (with hat, sunglasses and beard) at Hockenheim in 1980

05 Final preparations for Elio de Angelis' Lotus 81-Cosworth on the grid for the 1980 USAW GP at Long Beach

06 The Italian a year later at the same venue, driving the highly controversial twin-chassis type 88. During Saturday's practice, it was black-flagged and excluded from the race.

07 Third Lotus start for Nigel Mansell at Long Beach, in the 81B-Cosworth. The combative Briton had to retire after hitting a wall.

08 Formative year: Mansell at full throttle, Zandvoort, 1980, Lotus 81B-Cosworth. He spun off due to brake failure.

01 Flying the John Player banner again: Two mechanics working at the rear of Elio de Angelis' Lotus 87-Cosworth. The occasion is the 1981 French GP at Dijon-Prenois.

02 The Roman after hitting the Armco during a practice session at Zeltweg

03 On the scenic and mega-fast Styrian circuit, de Angelis came in seventh, one lap behind the winner Jacques Laffite.

the winner's circle, offering a foretaste of the much more successful 1977 campaign. This was the year that ground effect began to make its impact on Formula 1 in the attractive shape of the Lotus Type 78 (a.k.a. JPS Mk III). But although Andretti won more GPs in its cockpit than Niki Lauda at the wheel of the powerful Ferrari 312 T2, he eventually had to cede the title to the Austrian.

He was to make up for this emphatically in the following year, aboard the beautiful Lotus 79, whose greatly improved ground-effect aerodynamics laid much of the foundation of modern F1 thinking. Winning six rounds with that seemingly perfect tool Andretti delivered the team's last constructors' and drivers' titles. But again, disaster struck when he lost his popular team-mate and closest friend in the sport,

Ronnie Peterson, as a consequence of a multiple accident on the first lap of the Gran Premio d'Italia at Monza. Initially, the signs were encouraging as, amazingly, Peterson had only broken his legs. But then, on Monday morning, the Swede succumbed to fat embolism, scotching any joy that might have been felt by the American who had achieved his life's ambition.

The devastating superiority of the Lotus 79 was showcased once again when the somewhat rusty Frenchman Jean-Pierre Jarier, hired as a replacement for Peterson, placed it on pole for the final grand prix of the year at Montréal. But from then on, things went downhill. The 1979 Lotus Type 80 carried ground effect too far and the Type 81, a much more conventional interim design, returned only modest results in

1980. Second place for Elio de Angelis at Interlagos was its best performance. What happened had a touch of déjà-vu about it. As the McLaren M23 had been a refined Lotus 72, as it were, competitors Ligier and later Williams took up Chapman's ideas but also eradicated the weaknesses of the concept. And, astonishingly, there were some. As Peter Wright, the engineer behind it, later admitted, the 79 had "the torsional stiffness of a wet lettuce". So it could not really cope with the downforce it produced. The same went for the Type 80. The 1981 "twin-chassis" Lotus 88, preceded by a Type 86 test version the year before, was meant to circumvent the FISA's regulations that ruled out sliding skirts. Much to Chapman's dismay, it was to be banned by the Paris custodians of the regulations. Another innovation, however, had come to stay: the use of carbon fibre for the tub.

01 Nigel Mansell exiting the Zeltweg *Bosch-Kurve* in 1982, later to be let down by his engine, whereas his team-mate Elio de Angelis won the race. The Lotus 91's monocoque weighed around just 18 kg.

02 The short wheelbase version of the Type 91 at Monaco, lifting its right-hand wheels. The brakes were mounted outboard front and rear. Colin Chapman was not a fan of Martin Ogilvie's design.

03 Nigel Mansell at Dijon-Prenios in the Swiss GP. He finished eighth, one lap behind.

The black gold of the 20th century was also utilized for the 87 interim model, again the result of an otherwise rather conventional approach. On 15 August 1982, Colin Chapman flung his black cap into the air one last time at the Österreichring, when de Angelis beat Williams driver Keke Rosberg by a foot. The Italian drove the 91 model, which had evolved from the 87. Having come home from a FISA meeting in Paris on 16 December, Chapman died of a heart attack, at the age of only 54. Many said that he had overburdened himself when he became involved in the abortive De Lorean sports car project in 1978. Less prominent in his running of Team Lotus towards the end, his spirit was nevertheless indelibly imprinted on his team.

01 Brothers in arms: Nigel Mansell and Elio de Angelis at Hockenheim, 1983

02 The Lotus 94T-Renault, designed by Gérard Ducarouge, with its multi-layered rear wing at Zandvoort, same year

03 Bearing past laurels: Elio de Angelis at Hockenheim in the 95T-Renault, sporting the seven championships of the team in a suitable act of symbolism

01 Elio de Angelis and the 1994 model Lotus
   95T-Renault at Zandvoort and ...

02 ... Brands Hatch

03 The Principality at its worst: Nigel Mansell
   was leading the 1984 Monaco GP and
   heading for his first Formula 1 victory.
   But on lap 16, he was to crash heavily
   after a sideways slide behind St. Dévote.

Responsibility was taken over by Peter Warr. A year later, he hired French chassis designer Gérard Ducarouge, who created the Renault-engined type 94T in a couple of weeks, adapting 91 monocoques that had been redundant for two years. In 1984 de Angelis and Lotus finished third in both championships, in spite of not winning a single race. That changed with the advent of Ayrton Senna, who immediately made a splash with a sensational win in the rain at Estoril driving the 97T, followed by another triumph at Spa. De Angelis scored his second and last win at Imola. Then Senna gained two firsts in 1986 with the evolutionary 98T, his season burnished with eight pole positions.

At the end of the year the team lost its John Player & Sons backing. But Camel was already waiting in the wings.

01 De Angelis biding his time at Monaco in the Lotus 97T-Renault without…

02 … and with bodywork. Even the bare monocoque carries the JPS emblem. The year is 1985.

03 The 1.5 litre Renault turbo engine of the 97T, ready to deliver up to 1000 bhp (in practice trim)

04 Early masterpiece: At the 1985 Portuguese GP in Estoril, Ayrton Senna shrugs off torrential April rains and scores a splendid victory, never putting a wheel wrong.

05 At Silverstone in July, the 97T of Elio de Angelis is being completed. The bodywork visibly does not weigh much.

NEXT PAGE

01 Complex puzzle: Rear view of the Lotus 98T-Renault, Hockenheimring, 1986

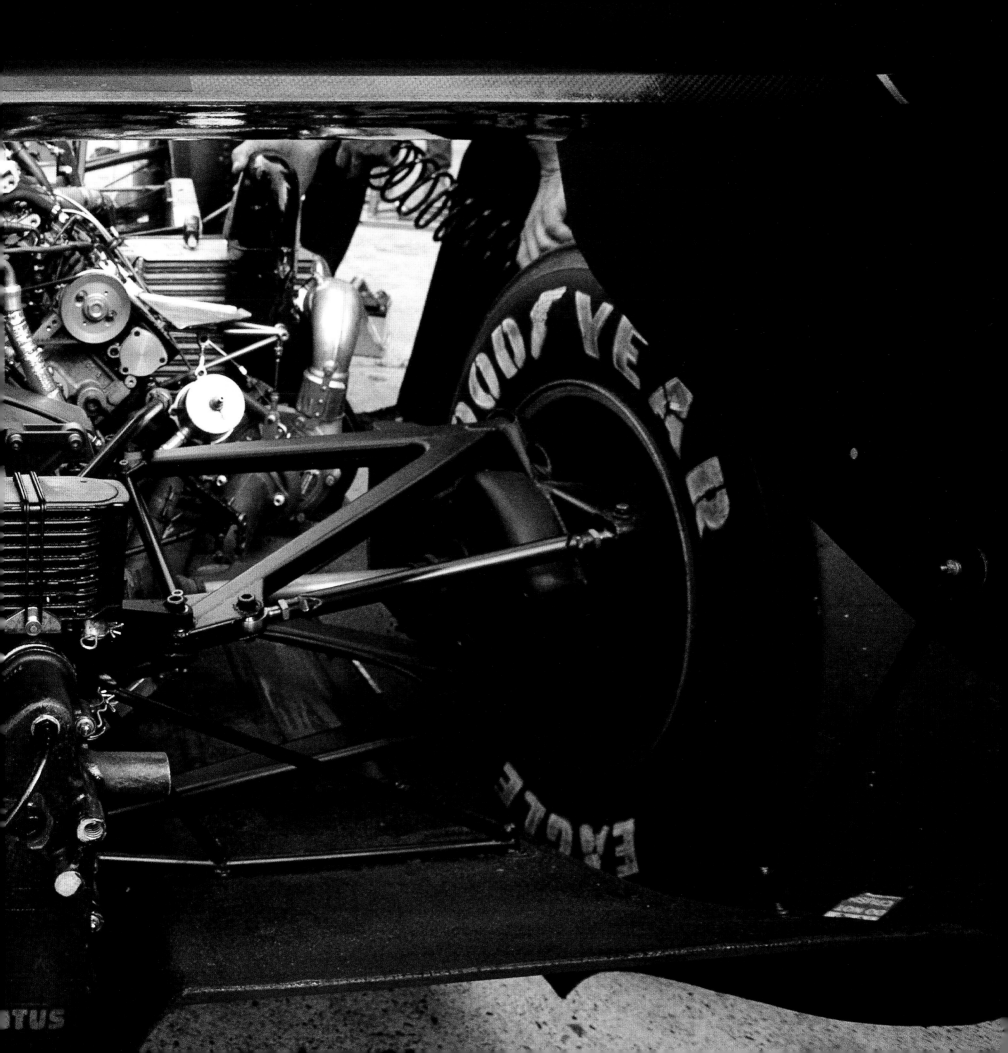

01 A shower of sparks as Senna's 98T touches down at the lowest point of the Österreichring's home straight

02 The left rear tyre of Senna's car still provides basic information.

03 The Brazilian during the German GP at the Hockenheimring in 1986, heading for second place behind compatriot Nelson Piquet

04 Conferences at Monza with pensive designer Gérard Ducarouge with…

05 … and without helmet. Senna's face tells it all.

NEXT PAGE

01 Practice shot of Ayrton Senna, Lotus 98T-Renault, Monza, 1986. The transmission will give up the ghost at the start.

4

CAMEL

CHANGE OF COLOURS:
CAMEL

FROM 1987 THROUGH TO 1990, LOTUS ENJOYED THE BENEFIT OF CAMEL BACKING. IN THE FIRST YEAR, TWO MORE VICTORIES WERE PROVIDED BY BRAZILIAN PRODIGY AYRTON SENNA. BUT THEREAFTER THE TEAM BEGAN TO SLIDE DOWNHILL. MATTERS WERE NOT IMPROVED BY PETER WARR'S DEPARTURE IN 1989.

1987-1990

YEAR	CARS	DRIVERS	GP VICTORIES
1987	Lotus 99T-Honda V6	Ayrton Senna / Satoru Nakajima	MON / USAE (both Senna)
1988	Lotus 100T-Honda V6	Nelson Piquet / Satoru Nakajima	—
1989	Lotus 101-Judd V8	Nelson Piquet / Satoru Nakajima	—
1990	Lotus 102-Lamborghini V12	Derek Warwick / Martin Donnelly / Johnny Herbert	—

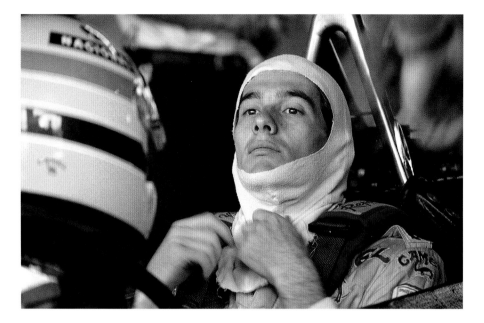

The 1987 curtain raiser at Jacarepagua saw the Lotus 99Ts rolled out of the transporter in the distinctive yellow and blue colours of new sponsor Camel. It looked as if the marque was heading for a new beginning. Senna's supreme talent had not gone unnoticed, attracting the attention of Honda. When Lotus agreed to employ Satoru Nakajima as its second driver, the deal was struck. The Japanese giant supplied the team with its 1.5-litre RA166-E turbocharged V6 unit, which was claimed to put out more than 1000 bhp in qualifying tune and 815 bhp during the race, paid for, however, with severe vibration. Unlike the Williams FW11Bs, which used the same engine and dominated that grand prix year, Senna's 99T sometimes ran very low on fuel.

Ducarouge's new chassis was basically the same as the predecessor's, but made much sturdier to cope with all that power. It was another attempt at computer-controlled

active suspension, a brainchild of Colin Chapman's as long ago as the early eighties, before his premature death. As in 1992, on the later Type 107, the system, used on Senna's insistence, was actuated at each corner by a hydraulic pressure pump. Nevertheless, the Brazilian secured just two wins for himself and the team, at Monaco (his first of a record-breaking six victories in the Principality) and at Detroit.

Senna departed at the end of the season, leaving a legacy of six of his 41 grand prix victories and the last for Team Lotus. The others were all scored in the services of new employer McLaren, who, in 1988, also enjoyed the benefit of the all-conquering Honda power plant. In his stead, double world champion Nelson Piquet joined the Hethel outfit, already seemingly in the downswing of his career and very much in the shadow of his up-and-coming compatriot Ayrton Senna. His own and the team's best placings were three thirds at the Brazilian and San Marino rounds at the

01 As he prepares for battle, Ayrton Senna already seems to be on a different planet, full of kerbs and brake points.

02 Team-mate in 1987 is Satoru Nakajima, whose best result will be fourth at Silverstone.

03 The Lotus 99T-Honda in its naked beauty, with Senna's yellow helmet on the front suspension

04 The car of Honda nominee Nakajima at the 1987 Hungarian GP, its powerful V6 fully exposed to curious views

05 The Japanese retired with drive shaft failure. At the Hungaroring, the 99Ts featured modified bodywork, with a lower and narrower cockpit surround, as well as lower side-pods.

06 Farewell performance: 1987 was Ayrton Senna's third and final Lotus year – on the threshold of an incomparable but tragic career.

07 All sound and fury: Ayrton Senna during the 1987 Monaco GP, en route towards a resounding victory, his first of six in the Principality

beginning of the 1988 season and at the finale in Adelaide. A little later, Ducarouge called it quits, patriotically opting to support the efforts of the new squad of fellow Frenchman Gérard Larrousse. His last Lotus chassis had been the needle-nosed yet aerodynamically deficient 100T, closely modelled on the 99T, but with conventional suspension by push-rods, double wishbones and inboard spring/damper units all round.

1989 saw drastic change, inasmuch as the era of the turbo monsters had come to an end, with the latest regulations stipulating normally aspirated 3.5-litre engines. No longer a Honda customer, Lotus had to opt for the 90-degree Judd CV V8, which produced about 610 bhp. It was combined with the customary longitudinal Lotus/Hewland six-speed transaxle. Like its two predecessors', the 99T and the 100T,

the 101's chassis was made of carbon/Kevlar composite. It was the work of former Williams aerodynamicist Frank Dernie, who had had to build it very quickly indeed.

The driver pairing of Piquet and Nakajima was in for a meagre year, with three fourth positions for the Brazilian, at Montréal, Silverstone and Suzuka the best that could be achieved. Neither driver managed to qualify for the Belgian GP, unheard-of in the history of the team. To make things worse, both team boss Peter Warr and chairman Fred Bushell left in mid-season, replaced by 66-year-old Tony Rudd, who was drafted in from Group Lotus.

In 1990 Lotus retained Camel sponsorship but had to persevere through yet another lean season. Dernie's Type 102 had evolved from the preceding year's car. It had to be

01 Nelson Piquet, Lotus 101-Judd, Hungaroring, 1989. Both the marque and the flamboyant Brazilian are now past their prime.

02 Ubiquitous message: Nelson Piquet at Imola, in yellow surroundings

adjusted to a novel engine, an 80-degree Lamborghini V12, largely the work of famous former Ferrari engineer Mauro Forghieri. It sounded beautiful and gave an optimistic 640 bhp but was long, heavy and thirsty, as well as causing aerodynamic problems. The T102 was driven by Derek Warwick and Martin Donnelly, their very best efforts rewarded with a spectacular somersault for Warwick at the Italian GP and a terrible accident for Donnelly at Jerez that put an end to the Irishman's F1 career after only 14 grands prix.

5

HITACHI

LAST BASTION:
HITACHI

THE FINAL CHAPTER OF THE LOTUS SAGA IN THE LAST CENTURY WAS MARKED BY FINANCIAL STRAITS LEADING TO INEVITABLE CONSEQUENCES, WITH FREQUENT CHANGES TO THE TEAM – DRIVERS INCLUDED. GOOD IDEAS THAT COULD NOT BE PERFECTED, AND A COMPLETE LACK OF SUCCESS AMOUNTED TO A VICIOUS CIRCLE.

1991-1994

YEAR	CARS	DRIVERS	GP VICTORIES
1991	Lotus 102B-Judd V8	Mika Häkkinen / Julian Bailey / Johnny Herbert / Michael Bartels	—
1992	Lotus 102D and 107-Ford HB V8	Mika Häkkinen / Johnny Herbert	—
1993	Lotus 107B-Ford HB V8	Johnny Herbert / Alex Zanardi / Pedro Lamy	—
1994	Lotus 107C-Ford HB V8 Lotus 109-Mugen-Honda V10	Johnny Herbert / Alex Zanardi / Pedro Lamy Philippe Adams / Eric Bernard / Mika Salo	—

01 The Judd V8 powering the 102B was no match for the Honda, Renault and Ferrari engines that dominated the 1991 season.

02 Mika Häkkinen, the latest "Flying Finn", ended up three laps behind winner Riccardo Patrese at Estoril in 1991.

03 This shot of Häkkinen at Monaco in the bare 102B-Judd epitomizes the team's inability to obtain adequate sponsorship.

04 Paradoxically, with the outfit in dire need, the Team Lotus logo is very much in evidence, here on Mika Häkkinen's 102B at Monaco.

In December 1990 the Lotus team was taken over by former employees Peter Collins and Peter Wright. Although, in time, they managed to obtain sponsorship from Hitachi, Castrol, Loctite and the American Miller Brewing Company, they still had to make do with a shoestring budget and consequently underwent a period full of trials and tribulations.

The initial driver pairing consisted of a young Mika Häkkinen and Londoner Julian Bailey, the latter being replaced by Johnny Herbert from Montréal onwards. However, Herbert missed four GPs because of Formula 3000 commitments, Michael Bartels failing to qualify as his temporary replacement. Their chassis, devoid of any major sponsorship and thus painfully naked, was basically the one-year-old Type 102,

slightly modified into 'B' specification, with an old Judd EV 76-degree V8 in the rear. Experienced ex-McLaren and Spirit designer Gordon Coppuck had a share in developing the concept. Fifth for Häkkinen and sixth for Bailey at Imola were the proverbial swallows that did not make a summer. The Finn failed to qualify only once, but retired seven times.

The T102 carried on into the 1992 season in 'D' guise, powered by a Ford HB engine which was no match for the Renault and Honda units. After the San Marino GP the 102D was replaced by the type 107, designed by Wright and Chris Murphy. The latest Lotus featured semi-active suspension. It resembled the system on the make's road cars, using an electronic ride-height control to keep ground clearance constant.

01 Johnny Herbert replaced Julian Bailey in Canada. After failing to qualify at Montréal, he made it onto the grid for all of the remaining 52 grands prix he drove for the team.

02 Mika Häkkinen hopping over the kerbs, Monaco, 1991

It could also be switched off, and its promise and real possibilities were never fully exploited. The 1992 campaign culminated in fourth and sixth finishes for Häkkinen and Herbert respectively at Magny-Cours.

Things seemed to be looking up for Lotus when the much improved type 107B was launched in London's famous Claridge's hotel in Mayfair. Herbert remained with the team, while Häkkinen had been superseded by the personable Italian Alex Zanardi. However, their progress was hampered by aerodynamic deficiencies, a faulty active suspension and the power deficit of the HB (series V) unit. During practice at Spa, Zanardi suffered a hair-raising accident at the notorious Eau Rouge section, an eerie silence descending on the severely injured driver and the scattered debris of his car.

For the remainder of the F1 season the young and inexperienced Portuguese Pedro Lamy was employed in his stead. The year was highlighted by three fourth places for Johnny Herbert, at Interlagos, Donington Park and Silverstone, a far cry from what had once been expected of the Lotus name.

In 1994 the team descended into desperate straits. The 107C run in the first four grands prix was an interim car, its Mugen-Honda 72-degree V10 driving through a new six-speed semi-automatic gearbox. The drivers at the beginning of the season were again Herbert and Lamy. But the Portuguese was sidelined by the serious injuries he sustained in a practice crash at Silverstone in May. His place was taken back by Zanardi, later to be dropped from the team twice in favour of the Belgian "pay

01 Häkkinen in the Lotus 107-Ford HB at Montréal in 1992. He retired, with his gearbox on strike.

02 The Finn at Barcelona, same year, still in the 102D-Ford HB. The team brought the first 107 to Spain but did not race it.

03 Team-mates Johnny Herbert and Mika Häkkinen having a chat

04 The struggle was to no avail: Retirement at Monaco for both Häkkinen (gearbox) and Herbert (accident)

05 Spidery appearance of the 102D at Monaco, the metal rims being employed for pit and paddock use only

driver" Philippe Adams, who was said to have pledged $500,000 to the cash-strapped squad. At the Spanish GP in May the T109 appeared, but it fared no better than its predecessor. There was a glimpse of hope at Monza, when Herbert qualified fourth with a stronger Honda ZA6C V10. But it was shattered in a multi-car crash on the first lap.

The day after the Italian GP, the team applied for an administration order. Its last race was the 1994 Australian Grand Prix.

01 Casual Lotus labourer Alex Zanardi in the T109 at Magny-Cours in 1994. The amiable Italian retired when he realized that his Mugen-Honda V10 was on fire.

02 Johnny Herbert at Monza, 1993, after crashing his 107B at the Parabolica

03 Parting shot, for the time being: Johnny Herbert heading for the Lotus pits at Hockenheim, 1993

6

LOTUS
RACING

6 · LOTUS RACING

COMING FULL CIRCLE: LOTUS RACING

THE MOTOR RACING WORLD OWES THE RENAISSANCE OF THE LOTUS LEGEND TO DYNAMIC MALAYSIAN BUSINESSMAN TONY FERNANDES. ONCE THE FIA HAD GIVEN THE NOD IN SEPTEMBER 2009, THE NEW T127 CHALLENGER WAS BUILT FROM A BLANK SHEET OF PAPER IN ONLY FIVE MONTHS. DURING THE 2010 CAMPAIGN THE ANGLO-MALAYSIAN SQUAD IMPRESSIVELY ACHIEVED THE TARGET SET BEFORE THE SEASON: TO BE THE BEST OF THE NEW TEAMS IN ITS MAIDEN YEAR.

2010

YEAR	CARS	DRIVERS	GP VICTORIES
2010	Lotus T127-Cosworth V8	Heikki Kovalainen / Jarno Trulli / Fairuz Fauzy	

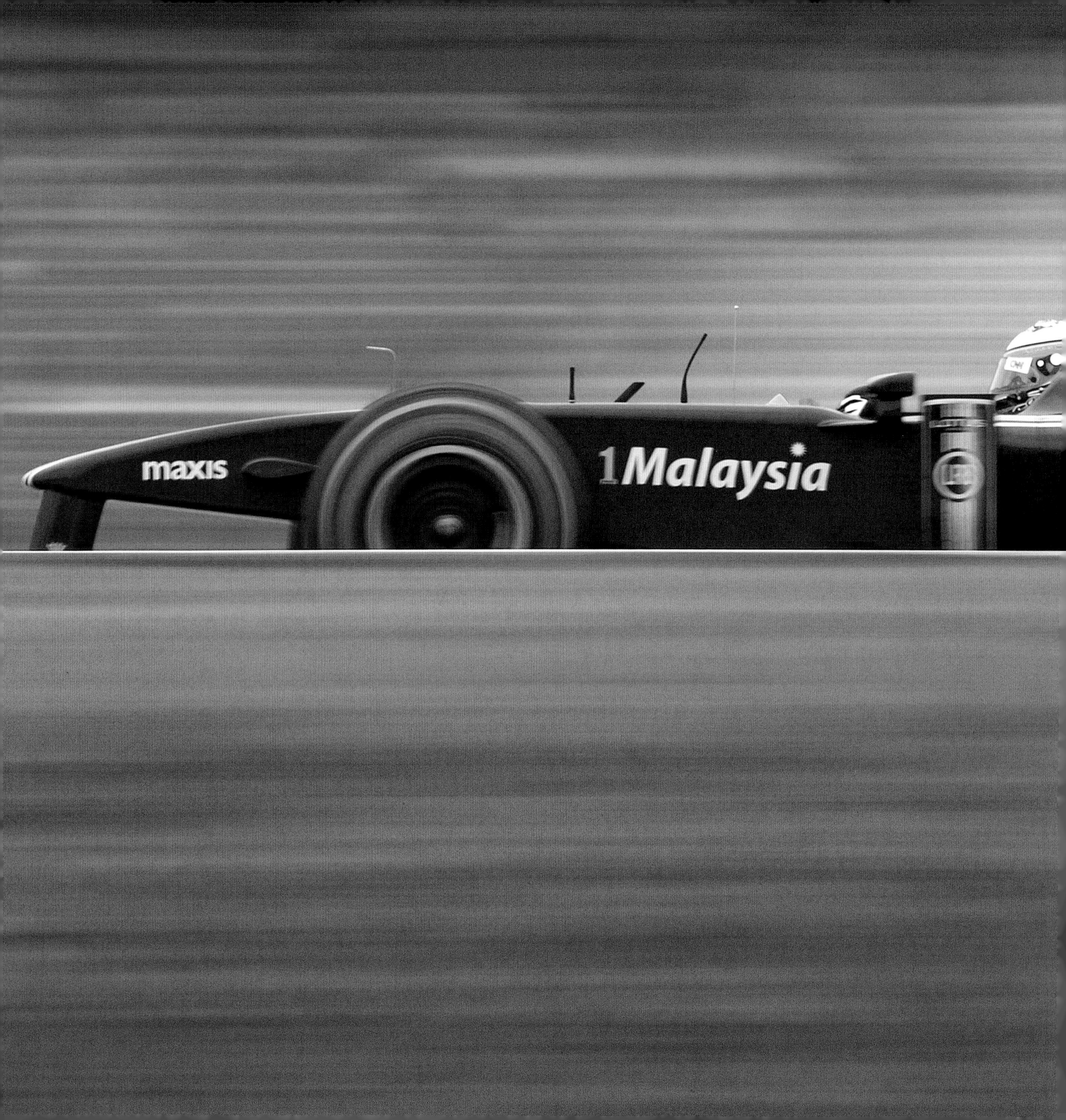
maxis
1Malaysia

O n 15 September 2009 the FIA announced that the Lotus marque would be returning to Formula 1. The man behind the new effort was successful Malaysian entrepreneur Tony Fernandes.

Using the name's mystique as a medium, Tony wanted to transcend the fences of the Global Village, with one base in Hingham, not far from Hethel, and another in Kuala Lumpur, very far away indeed. He enthusiastically spoke about opening up the sport to a whole new audience, both geographically and demographically. He started building a Malaysian consortium, including the country's government and Proton, the owner of Lotus Cars. Sceptics needed to be convinced that Lotus Racing was the spiritual successor to Team Lotus, one of the grandest names in grand prix racing. The support of the Chapman family had to be secured.

01 Bahrain: A dream start for Lotus Racing, with both cars finishing the race

02 Istanbul: Jarno Trulli has to retire with hydraulics failure, and so does Heikki Kovalainen.

03 Bahrain, and no problems at all for Kovalainen. Team boss Tony Fernandes is "over the moon".

04 Barcelona: The Finn is delighted, as the new updates work immediately, improving high speed stability. But trouble with the gearbox software makes him redundant on race Sunday.

05 Sepang: Truncated race for Trulli after a tangle with Virgin man Timo Glock

06 Reunion with a glorious past: Classic Team Lotus Festival at Snetterton in June 2010 with Clive Chapman, Heikki Kovalainen, the Lotus 18, Jarno Trulli and Mike Gascoyne

07 Silverstone: 17th position for Kovalainen, who could not really push on through dense traffic

08 Valencia: The T127 ready to go, but not a good weekend for Lotus with Trulli 21st and Kovalainen involved in an accident with Mark Webber

09 Shanghai: Pit stop for Trulli who will be sidelined with hydraulics trouble

10 Imbued with passion and resolution: Lotus Racing Supremo Tony Fernandes

What then followed was a success story in itself, worthy of the Lotus legend. Within five months a team was set up from scratch, a factory established and a workforce of 140 specialists recruited, headed by experienced designer Mike Gascoyne, who had just been dreaming of taking a sabbatical from the demanding business of Formula 1 and sailing around the world. The car they built was along conventional lines, but fast enough to beat the other two newcomers to F1. In keeping with tradition, its designation was the T127 and it featured a Cosworth engine like so many of its predecessors, as well as an Xtrac gearbox.

On 12 February 2010 the spick-and-span, green and yellow projectile was unveiled in London's *Royal Horticultural Hall,* after a short shakedown run with Malaysian rookie Fairuz Fauzy at the wheel two days earlier at Silverstone. The Chapmans

01 Sepang: Noisy torso of the T127

02 Sepang: Eventful race for Kovalainen on a wet Sepang circuit. A rear left tyre puncture after a tussle with Virgin driver de Grassi, high temperatures, slight hydraulics issues, but competitive all the same

and the three smiling drivers Fauzy, Jarno Trulli and Heikki Kovalainen were all in attendance. Mike Gascoyne admitted that the months just passed had been the most challenging of his career.

On 23rd February 2010 Tun Dr. Mahathir Mohamad, the former Prime Minister of Malaysia, opened the team's Hingham base. After encouraging winter tests which bore testimony to the car's pace and reliability, both Lotus T127s raced past the chequered flag in the season's opening round in the heat of Bahrain. Kovalainen came in 15th and Trulli 17th, whilst neither of the other two new teams lasted more than 28 of the 49 laps. One of the Renaults and both Sauber cars also failed to make the finish.

Not only did that race weekend see 18 of the sport's world champions who are still with us come together, including ex-Lotus men Fittipaldi and Andretti and their erstwhile vehicles, but also a moving reunion of former Lotus staff members, Peter Warr among them. Colin Chapman would have been proud of the team's achievement, he said. Chapman's cap, presented to Tony Fernandes before the race, came in a box with a message attached: "For when next needed."

But Rome wasn't built in a day. For the time being, a message released by the alert Lotus Racing press officer Tom Webb for the Italian GP on 12 September 2010 said it all: "It's already been an incredible 365 days, and we have more exciting days to come."

01 Monza: Good start for Jarno Trulli, a comfortable lead in the new teams' league, but gearbox failure on lap 46

02 Shanghai: 14th place secured by Kovalainen, owing to the right tyre choice in tricky weather conditions

03 Fully prepared for the grand prix: Heikki Kovalainen

NEXT PAGE
01 Barcelona: Practice shot of Heikki Kovalainen

02 Monaco: Jarno Trulli would not finish the GP in the Principality because of a spectacular slow motion crash with Karun Chandhok's HRT in the dying moments of the race. But here he is seen at speed, entering *Massenet* corner.

This was indeed so, even after SM Nasarudin, Kamarudin Meranun and Tony Fernandes, the three shareholders of Lotus Racing, had proclaimed a fortnight later what they had been dreaming of from the outset: the squad would be rebranded Team Lotus in 2011.

Noblesse oblige – the threesome was certainly aware of the implications …

01 Budapest: Jarno Trulli leaving the pit. In the race he has to let his team-mate go first because of safety car topsy-turvydom.

02 Budapest: Preparing for another race that will consolidate the Lotus leadership among the new teams

03 Monza: The calm before the storm. There is also a world beyond Formula 1 racing.

04 Silverstone: Another two car finish for the team, with Trulli leading home Kovalainen. Somewhere, VIP guest Hazel Chapman, Colin's widow, is watching.

05 Budapest: A Lotus T127 waiting to be let loose

NEXT PAGE:
06 Monaco: Light at the end of the tunnel. But Heikki Kovalainen has to apply maximum lock in right-hand corners because of uneven steering alignment.

WINNERS:
EIGHT LOTUS
DRIVERS

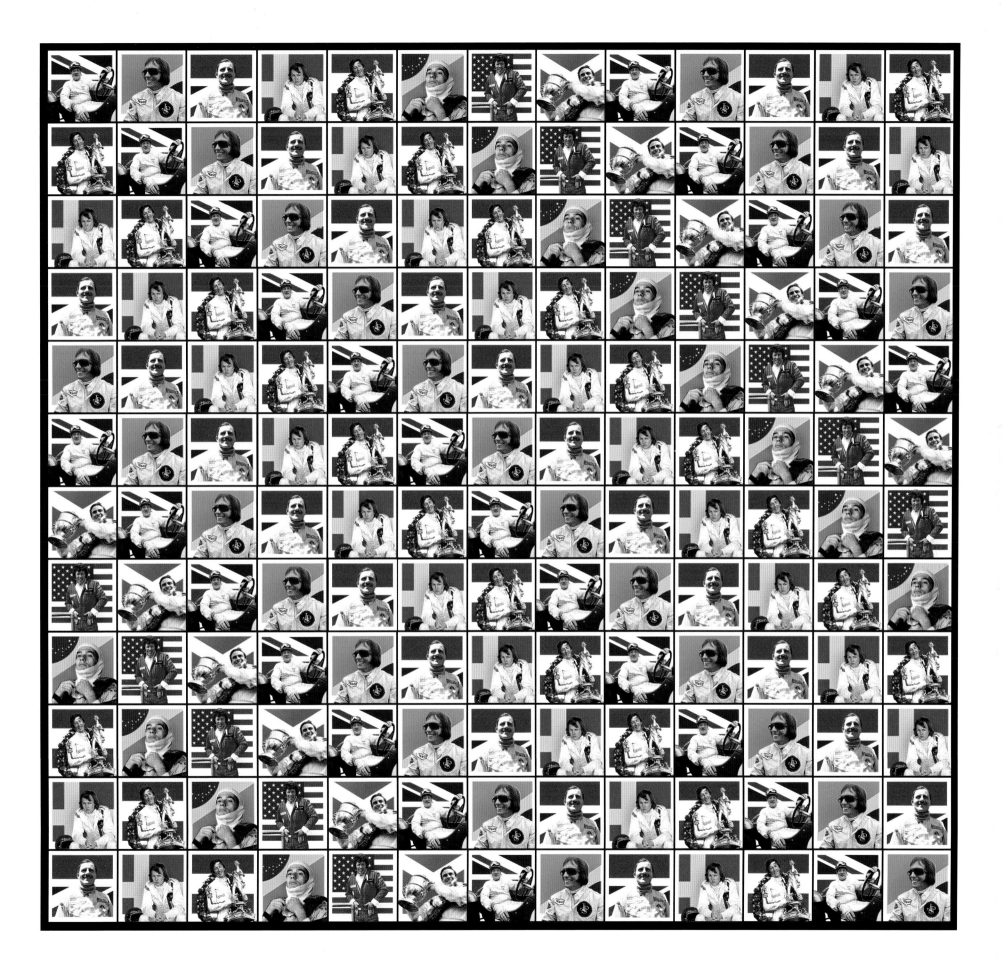

STIRLING MOSS UNCROWNED KING

LOTUS YEARS	1960–61
GRANDS PRIX	12*
VICTORIES	4*
BEST WORLD CHAMPIONSHIP PLACING	3 (1960, 1961)*
WINNING CARS	LOTUS 18-CLIMAX 4
	LOTUS 18/21-CLIMAX 4

* DRIVING ROB WALKER'S LOTUSES

Stirling Moss – there is something to those three syllables in terms of sound and rhythm. But even without such magical language Moss, born in London on 17 September 1929, would have made a name for himself, a permanent star in the galaxy of racing drivers that has lost little of its radiance up to the present day. With 16 victories and pole positions, as well as 19 fastest laps in 66 grands prix to his credit, he also chalked up innumerable successes in other categories, each one rich in charisma. "Stirling alone is worth a second per lap," Count Wolfgang Berghe von Trips used to say about him.

But the quality label Moss wore carried the blemish that he was "the greatest driver never to have won a world championship". Between 1955 and 1958 he kept finishing as runner-up in the final standings, and from 1959 to 1961 in third position. In 1958 the title seemed within touching distance. That season, in the finale at Casablanca, the fervently patriotic Moss would have achieved his life's ambition in a British car, the Vanwall, had not Ferrari novice Phil Hill waved through his team-mate Mike Hawthorn to become 1958 champion.

Moss had joined the mighty Mercedes squad in 1955. That he won his home grand prix at Aintree, with his master, disciplinarian and undisputed number one in the Mercedes squad, Fangio, breathing down his neck, always left him a little suspicious. Had that victory not been handed to him on a silver plate by the enigmatic Argentinian, a grand gesture for services rendered in the past when Moss had backed him up so efficiently? He did, however, prevail over Fangio in the two-seater racing car. His victory in the 1955 Mille Miglia, at the wheel of the all-conquering Mercedes-Benz 300 SLR, ably supported by the tiny and tough bearded journalist Denis Jenkinson as a sort of war correspondent, was not least a triumph over the fervently revered Fangio. Time and again Ferrari held out rosy prospects to Moss. But he preferred the warmth and security afforded by the private racing stable of abstemious whisky heir, fatherly pedagogue, gentleman and friend, Rob Walker to a comparatively chaotic and complex Italian organization. In doing so, he also deliberately opted for the part of the underdog, a role in which Moss revelled and which brought him some of his most rewarding feats, such as victories in the 1961 Monaco and German grands prix over the vastly superior Ferraris in Walker's Lotus 18 and 18/21.

A terrible accident at Goodwood put an end to his brilliant career in 1962. Before he had completely recovered and still unable to walk properly, he sat at the wheel of a Lotus two-seater sports racing car for tests, again at Goodwood. The result was shattering, at least in Moss' view. His reflexes were as good as they used to be. But he could not concentrate any longer the way a racing driver has to. "Who does not drive fast and safely," he said, "ought to throw in the towel, if only out of consideration for his competitors."

JIM CLARK
THE GOOD
SHEPHERD

LOTUS YEARS   1960–68
GRANDS PRIX   72
VICTORIES   25
TITLES   2 (1963, 1965)
WINNING CARS: LOTUS 25-CLIMAX V8
LOTUS 33-CLIMAX V8
LOTUS 49-COSWORTH V8

The morning of 7 April 1968 was overcast and rainy. After the fourth lap of the first part of the Hockenheim Formula 2 race for the *Deutschlandtrophäe,* one car went missing. An ambulance drove onto the circuit. Soon afterwards, the terrible news began to spread in the paddock, very slowly but almost physically palpable, wherever people stood together. Some wept, others embraced or just cast their eyes down.

The spectators were only informed at the beginning of the second heat, when the cars were approaching the stadium again for the first time, their engines screaming. "Jim Clark is dead," blared the loudspeakers, the commentator somehow oddly indulging in the theatricality of the situation. "Let's rise from our seats. But the race goes on." Somewhere in the absurd solitude of the Hockenheim forest straights, the destruction of the seemingly indestructible had taken place. The sport had lost the dominant driver personality of the sixties between slender trees. Nobody had seen the accident.

As his friend, jazz trombonist Chris Barber, puts it, Clark seemed to be everybody's darling, even though he left them standing at will. Just 32, world champion in 1963 and 1965 as well as an Indy victor in 1965, he had won 25 of his 72 grands prix. He had amassed 33 pole positions and 28 fastest laps like the fruits grown in a field on his Edington Mains farm, near Duns in Scotland, where he had been brought up with loving care, looked after and pampered by his four elder sisters. He never ceased being a farmer in his heart. "When I left school at sixteen, my father gave me a dog and a

stick and just asked me to carry on. Everything seemed to be predestined," he used to say. But that did not prevent him from discovering the glitter on the other side of the fence, as fellow Lotus driver Innes Ireland later said about him, with a residence in Bermuda and, from 1967, the Paris apartment he shared with French journalist Jabby Crombac.

Colin Chapman was both the man who provided him with the cars that matched his talent and his soulmate, his alter ego. They even competed against one another, as at the traditional grand finale of the season in Brands Hatch on 26 December 1958, driving works Elites. Their admiration was mutual: "I was at once impressed by the way Colin calmly assessed a situation, immediately taking the right decision," enthused Clark, after Chapman had directed the Scot and the bearded Sir John Whitmore into tenth place at Le Mans in 1959 in a Lotus Elite. And: "Jimmy is an exceptional character who would succeed in any sport," came the response. But Chapman also made the point that Clark doggedly stuck to his opinions, having a brilliant memory for the things he was prepared to remember.

He also was the first of a new breed of drivers making a career of racing. "In our time there is no more room for yesterday's colourful characters," was his creed. "Today's drivers are young and uncompromising, products of the technical age." But, alas, the Hockenheim safety standards had not kept pace.

GRAHAM HILL THE MUSTACHIOED LONDONER

LOTUS YEARS	1958–59, 1967–70
GRANDS PRIX	60*
VICTORIES	4*
TITLES	1 (1968)*
WINNING CARS	LOTUS 49-COSWORTH V8
	LOTUS 49B-COSWORTH V8

* IN LOTUS SERVICES

Before each European grand prix of the 1975 season an anonymous caller rang up Embassy Racing: "Will Graham start?" he wanted to know. The answer was always the same: "No, he will be concentrating on his function as team boss." "Then I won't go," said the man. He was just one of many aficionados of the popular Londoner and as stubbornly true, although Hill, born in 1929 under the sign of Aquarius as the son of a stockbroker, was certainly no longer the driver he used to be.

He had risen from scratch, imbued with ambition and sheer tenacity, eventually far exceeding the critical 40-year barrier and growing into the honourable role of a worthy ambassador for his sport. He had diced with death for more than a quarter of a century, travelling in the narrow border zone between being and not being for hundreds of thousands of kilometres. While, in his seven seasons with BRM (1960-1966), he was on the whole spared mechanical defects, his Lotus years were marked by drama, endured with stoic composure. Already in his first grand prix, Monaco in 1958, a rear wheel of his Lotus 12 sheared off. At the 1969 Spanish Grand Prix the rear wing of his white, red and gold 49B folded, having crested the infamous rise after the pits complex of the Montjuich Park circuit. The car hammered into the Armco, Hill emerging from the wreck unscathed.

Five months later, in Watkins Glen, he had to push-start his vehicle after a spin. Unable to fasten his seatbelts, he spun again. This time the car overturned and he was thrown out, breaking his two legs and severely damaging his knees. His only aim, though, was to be on the grid for the South African Grand Prix another five months later. And indeed he managed to score a point in Kyalami at the wheel of Rob Walker's blue and white Lotus 49C. But only rarely did the old tiger bare his teeth thereafter.

He could be proud of what he had achieved anyway, his mere statistics making fascinating reading. Graham Hill took part in 176 grand prix races, won 14 of them, and was world champion in 1962 and 1968. Between 1963 and 1965 there was a remarkable symmetry to his balance sheet: second in the final standings behind Jim Clark, John Surtees and again Clark, victories in Monaco and Watkins Glen, as if he had subscribed to them. After he had paced up the red carpet to the stand of Prince Rainier III on a further two occasions in 1968 and 1969, the media crowned him King of Monaco. Triumphs in races as different as Indianapolis (in 1966 in a Lola) and Le Mans (in 1972 at the wheel of a Matra 670) rounded off a perfect career. It was only in 1975, however, that he finally decided to hang up his famous helmet in the black and white colours of his London rowing club.

That he should be killed in a plane crash the same year came as an ironically cruel twist of fate. He was on his way back from testing in Le Castellet, but perished with members of his team including rising star Tony Brise. His Piper Aztec had clipped a row of trees near the Elstree airfield in dense fog.

JOCHEN RINDT AUSTRIAN HERO

LOTUS YEARS	1969–70
GRANDS PRIX	19*
VICTORIES	6*
TITLES	1 (1970)*
WINNING CARS	LOTUS 49B-COSWORTH V8
	LOTUS 49C-COSWORTH V8
	LOTUS 72-COSWORTH V8

* IN LOTUS SERVICES

On his way to the grid of the *Rheinpokal* race for Formula 2 cars on 16 June 1968, he performed a full pirouette on the Hockenheim finishing straight, vulcanising a bold black circle on the track. The grandstands erupted with noisy approval.

That's how Jochen Rindt was. Born in Mainz on 18 April 1942, but an adopted Austrian, he brought colour and fire to his high-speed profession, a showman at the wheel who drove for the sheer joy. If a little cash came his way, so much the better. In the second half of the sixties he was anointed King of Formula 2. These nimble single-seaters were tailor-made for his slim stature, almost part of his body language. In 1967 alone, he notched up nine victories and four runner-up spots from 15 starts in the immaculately prepared Brabham of the Roy Winkelmann outfit, always entertaining the spectators with a flamboyant driving style as bold as his looks.

He also stood out because of his versatility. Rindt was a master of drift, whether in a saloon or a sports car, in Formula 2 or Formula 1. In June 1965, for instance, he won the Le Mans 24 hours, together with bespectacled American Masten Gregory, in the Ferrari 275 LM of the North American Racing Team. Two weeks later, he emerged a supreme winner ahead of Frank Gardner, Jim Clark, Alan Rees and Jackie Stewart in the F2 Brabham after an epic 300-kilometre slipstreamer in Reims. His drive in the French Grand Prix at Clermont-Ferrand in a Cooper-Climax on the preceding weekend had crashed to a premature end. He also failed to see the chequered flag in the British GP two weeks later, due to an engine failure. The Cooper-Maserati he drove in 1966 and 1967 was overweight and underpowered. Rindt tried in vain to bend that unwieldy piece of machinery to his will, his path littered with the wreckage of cars. But his courage and daring remained undiminished. In the rain-soaked 1966 Belgian GP at Spa, impressively documented in John Frankenheimer's cult film *Grand Prix,* the Cooper spun in the infamous Masta kink at full throttle, miraculously staying on the racing line. Completely unfazed, Rindt carried on to finish runner-up behind John Surtees, who drove his last race for Ferrari on that day.

In 1969, Jochen Rindt signed for Lotus. From then on, events unfolded as if following a script. In six victories, starting at Watkins Glen in the autumn of that year, he finally showed what he was made of. At Monaco on 10 May 1970 he gave a demonstration of imperious motoring for an hour, pressuring the old warhorse Jack Brabham into the straw bales at literally the last corner of the race. In Barcelona he crashed after his rear aerofoil had collapsed. He was fortunate to escape with a couple of cuts and bruises and a broken nose.

Not so in Monza on 5 September, while practising for the Italian GP. The right front brake shaft failed on his Lotus 72 at the Parabolica. Rindt died on his way to hospital. That year, Formula 1 would have the macabre attraction of a world champion who would never be able to enjoy the achievement.

EMERSON FITTIPALDI
WHIZZKID

LOTUS YEARS	1970–73
GRANDS PRIX	42*
VICTORIES	9*
TITLES	1 (1972)*
WINNING CARS	LOTUS 72C-COSWORTH V8
	LOTUS 72D-COSWORTH V8
	LOTUS 72E-COSWORTH V8

* IN LOTUS SERVICES

One of motor racing's Mozarts, Emerson Fittipaldi burst onto the Formula 1 scene at the 1970 British GP, having stormed through the minor formulae like a whirlwind. Born in São Paulo in 1946, he had arrived in England in May 1969, ambition in abundance, a load of cash and Frank Williams' address in his pocket.

His supreme talent did not go unnoticed. Which is why he enjoyed the benefit of support and patronage of racing greats such as Stirling Moss and influential Ford PR boss Walter Hayes, one of the men behind the DFV engine.

Fittipaldi then embarked upon a most unusual *curriculum vitae*. He won his fourth grand prix, in Watkins Glen, which was to usher in another 13 victories, and became the youngest world champion up to that point in 1972 at the tender age of 25, driving the D metamorphosis of the Lotus 72. This was all the more remarkable in that Lotus and Colin Chapman in particular had been badly shaken by Jochen Rindt's fatal accident at Monza in September 1970. The team threatened to fall apart. Chief designer Maurice Philippe had already resigned, and so had a number of mechanics. Both Emerson and his wife Maria Helena were severely injured in a road accident in France, which prevented him from taking part in the 1971 Zandvoort round of the championship. His 1972 crown was gained with comparative ease and occasional spots of good fortune. But by and large his victories were earned the hard way, the Brazilian and the Ford-powered black and gold JPS emerging as the most formidable partnership of the year. The respected English publication "Motor Racing Year" also hailed him as an asset to the sport as a whole: "His immense charm, good manners and quiet dignity will make him a fine ambassador for motor racing, as well as for his country."

In 1973, Lotus' strength also turned out to be a weakness as the premium driver pairing of Emerson Fittipaldi and Ronnie Peterson kept taking points away from one another, allowing Jackie Stewart to score his third world championship in a Tyrrell. Fittipaldi won in Buenos Aires, Interlagos and Barcelona, finishing as runner-up behind the Scotsman, while the Swede ended up in third position in the final standings.

"Fitti" claimed his second title in 1974 in a McLaren M23. He stayed with the Colnbrook outfit for a further year, but to everybody's amazement, either ill-advised or swayed by his patriotism, he made up his mind to join the Copersucar team run by his brother Wilson. This step seemed to diminish his brilliance and certainly made him an also-ran in the highest echelon of the sport. In 1981 he retired from driving but in 1984, he suddenly rediscovered in IndyCar racing what he had felt had gone forever in Formula 1: his old fire. In 1989 he won the PPG IndyCar World Series and the Indy 500, a feat that he was to repeat in 1993 after a duel with reigning F1-champion Nigel Mansell.

A horrific crash at the Michigan Speedway in July 1996 put an end to his racing career – apart from the odd appearance in historic events.

RONNIE PETERSON SUPER SWEDE

LOTUS YEARS	1973–76, 1978
GRANDS PRIX	59*
VICTORIES	9*
BEST WORLD CHAMPIONSHIP PLACING	2 (1978)*
WINNING CARS	LOTUS 72E-COSWORTH V8
	LOTUS 78-COSWORTH V8
	LOTUS 79-COSWORTH V8

* IN LOTUS SERVICES

Appearances can be deceptive. Ronnie Peterson, born in Örebro in February 1944, looked introverted, sometimes sullen, like a boy who had grown up too fast. But let loose in a racing car the blond Swede suddenly changed into a fiery entertainer in the mould of Jochen Rindt before him and Gilles Villeneuve after him. The crowd adored him because he provided them with exactly what they wanted to see. He was completely fearless, the latest of the late brakers. He rounded corners at angles that bordered on the absurd. His car control became legendary.

As would later be the case with Nelson Piquet and Chico Serra or Mika Häkkinen and Mika Salo, Ronnie had to overcome the staunch resistance of a compatriot, Reine Wisell, on his way to the top. After winning the blue riband Formula 3 event in Monaco in 1969 he was offered a three-year March contract, beginning with a season in the yellow type 701 entered by collector Colin Crabbe's Antique Automobiles Racing Team and in the new marque's Formula 2 type 702. His exploits, particularly in these small and wieldy single-seaters, turned out to be a revelation. In 1971, as a full works driver now, he became European Formula 2 champion winning five races out of eleven.

In 1973 Peterson joined Lotus, paired with Emerson Fittipaldi. He recommended himself with four victories in the French, Austrian, Italian and US grands prix in the second half of that season. Soon, his blue helmet protruding from the cockpit of the black and gold cars became a familiar sight. Ronnie impressed with another three wins at Monaco, Dijon and Monza during the 1974 season in the ageing Lotus 72E as the new 76 model failed to live up to expectations. His defection, as it was seen by the men at Bicester, did not go down well. For a long time, March designer Robin Herd fuelled his grudge against the JPS superstar by gazing at a photo opposite his desk in his office. It showed Ronnie and Colin Chapman shaking hands, laughing.

But that did not prevent Herd and Max Mosley from calling on Peterson's services again in 1976. The rapid Swede returned the favour in the shape of a brilliant win in the Italian Grand Prix after qualifying in only eighth position.

The following season he drove the Tyrrell six-wheeler P34, which, however, did not suit his exuberant and tail-happy driving style. Again and again he was outpaced by fellow Tyrrell driver Patrick Depailler. Some said Ronnie Peterson had lost his old panache.

But then came the 1978 season. Chapman took him back to drive the all-conquering 78 and 79 models, albeit strictly as number two to Mario Andretti. Ronnie, sometimes visibly quicker than his team-mate but kept behind by the orders from behind the pit wall, scored two more firsts in Kyalami and Zeltweg. His death, in the aftermath of a multiple first-lap accident in Monza on 10 September of that year, severely shook the motor racing community. His beautiful wife Barbro never recovered from the loss.

MARIO ANDRETTI
MISSION ACCOMPLISHED

LOTUS YEARS	1968–69, 1976–80
GRANDS PRIX	79*
VICTORIES	11*
TITLES	1 (1978)*
WINNING CARS	LOTUS 77-COSWORTH V8
	LOTUS 78-COSWORTH V8
	LOTUS 79-COSWORTH V8

* IN LOTUS SERVICES

There are many ways to translate the American Dream into reality. But Mario Andretti's approach was certainly unique. He couches it in a simple sentence: "I was born to be a racing driver." His proudest day, though, Andretti considers to have been 15 April 1964: "That's when I became a US citizen."

He came from Montona, Italy, and might have been the next Alberto Ascari, whom he adored. But after a dismal childhood, the Andrettis emigrated to the Land of Limitless Opportunity in 1955. Based in Nazareth, Texas, Mario soon began to take the motor racing world by storm, becoming the greatest all-rounder the sport has ever seen. His mantra is, and always has been: "If you wait, all that happens is that you get older." With specialization long since prevailing on the various battlefields of competition driving, his achievements will never be surpassed: 52 victories in IndyCars, pole position in his very first Formula 1 race at Watkins Glen in 1968 driving a Lotus, 18 pole positions and twelve wins out of 128 grand prix starts, 3577 kilometres in the lead, world champion in 1978 in Colin Chapman's 78 and 79 'wing cars'. In 1967 he was winner of the most prestigious NASCAR race, the Daytona 500, and secured three overall victories in the Sebring 12 Hours as well as fastest time in the 1969 Pikes Peak International Hill Climb.

He drove IndyCars for 30 years between 1965 and 1994, when he officially ended his career in the shape of the *Arrivederci Mario Tour*. Four times, in 1965, 1966, 1969 and 1984, the man from Nazareth emerged as IndyCar champion. But only once in a total of 19 starts, much to his chagrin, did he win the blue riband Indianapolis 500. And yet another feather is missing in Andretti's cap. Unlike Graham Hill, who had two Formula 1 titles and triumphs in Indy and Le Mans to his credit, Mario never managed to notch up victory at Le Mans, second (in 1995 in a Cougar C34 Porsche) being his best placing in the Sarthe classic. Needless to say, he sublimated his life-long passion for racing into a fortune, beginning as early as the sixties, when the likes of petrol additive producer STP, Ford and Firestone turned him into a millionaire.

The pundits of the sport still ponder what might have been if Mario Andretti had not commuted between the continents of the motor racing cosmos, focussing his talent on Formula 1 instead. He won his first grand prix, at Kyalami in 1971, in a Ferrari and his last, in his championship year 1978, in Zandvoort at the wheel of a Lotus. Mario had got the squad back on track in 1976 when the team seemed to have lost its way. He stayed with Lotus full-time until 1980, although he regarded his relationship with Chapman as "purely businesslike".

Figurehead of a motor racing dynasty and recently turned 70, Andretti showed up at the meeting of former Formula 1 champions in Bahrain in March 2010. He looked spry, spick-and-span and simply happy. His doctor had told him that, if he wanted, he could still race and keep up with the young ones.

AYRTON SENNA DRIVING TO PERFECTION

LOTUS YEARS	1985–87
GRANDS PRIX	48*
VICTORIES	6*
BEST WORLD CHAMPIONSHIP PLACING	3 (1987)*
WINNING CARS	LOTUS 97T-RENAULT V6
	LOTUS 98T-RENAULT V6
	LOTUS 99T-HONDA V6

* IN LOTUS SERVICES

"Who is the greatest among the drivers of this epoch?" Until 1 May 1994, this question would have been received with a mocking smile and the inevitable answer: "Senna of course."

There was no doubt about that, and the man himself, born in São Paulo in March 1960, also knew it.

It could be read in his face, in which a certain inscrutability and the unbridled will to win manifested themselves. He proved the latter often enough, gaining three titles in 1988, 1990 and 1991 and 41 grand prix victories, with an amazing 13,645 kilometres spent in the lead. His 65 pole positions bore witness to his capability to squeeze his exceptional powers of concentration into those one and a half minutes that really counted in the qualification rush hour. Then Ayrton Senna rose beyond himself and sometimes beyond the imaginable, as in that legendary pole lap at Monaco in 1988.

His genius already flared up in the opening race on the new Nürburgring on 5 May 1984, when the young and hitherto almost unknown Brazilian vanquished legends of this sport such as James Hunt, Niki Lauda, Alain Prost, Keke Rosberg and John Surtees in the rapid little Mercedes-Benz 190 E 2.3-16. A month later, everybody knew his name. As rains of biblical proportions hammered down onto the Monaco Principality he had been poised to challenge Prost for the lead in the unwieldy and difficult-to-drive Toleman when, controversially, the race was stopped. Senna would go on to win that event six times.

His skills in the wet shone again when he secured his first grand prix victory, at Estoril a year later, amidst icy April showers. Had somebody laid an *escudo* on the ideal line that day, Senna's black and gold Lotus would have gone over it every lap. His father Milton had bought him out of his Toleman contract with 100,000 pounds sterling. Lotus offered him more chances to realize his ambition between 1985 and 1987. But his time with the Hethel squad was a foretaste of greater things to come, rather than the breakthrough he sought. Nevertheless, he presented himself, as well as team boss Peter Warr, with five more victories before he left for McLaren, taking a Honda engine contract with him.

Whenever somebody challenged his dominance Senna would inevitably get to grips with them, armoured by the unyielding carbon fibre cocoon of his cars. At Spa, he and Nigel Mansell left the track in discord in 1987, both having claimed the same piece of road at the same time. The 1989 and 1990 world championships were decided at Suzuka in scuffles with Alain Prost, Ayrton even intimating to a group of friends where he was going to launch his attack in the first of those years, when the two were still driving for McLaren.

Whom the gods love die young. They must have loved Ayrton Senna, who was a firm and avowed believer, in particular. Soon after his crash in Imola on that Sunday in May 1994, the body language of FIA doctor Sid Watkins betrayed the whole extent of the tragedy. The gap that Senna left would never be filled.

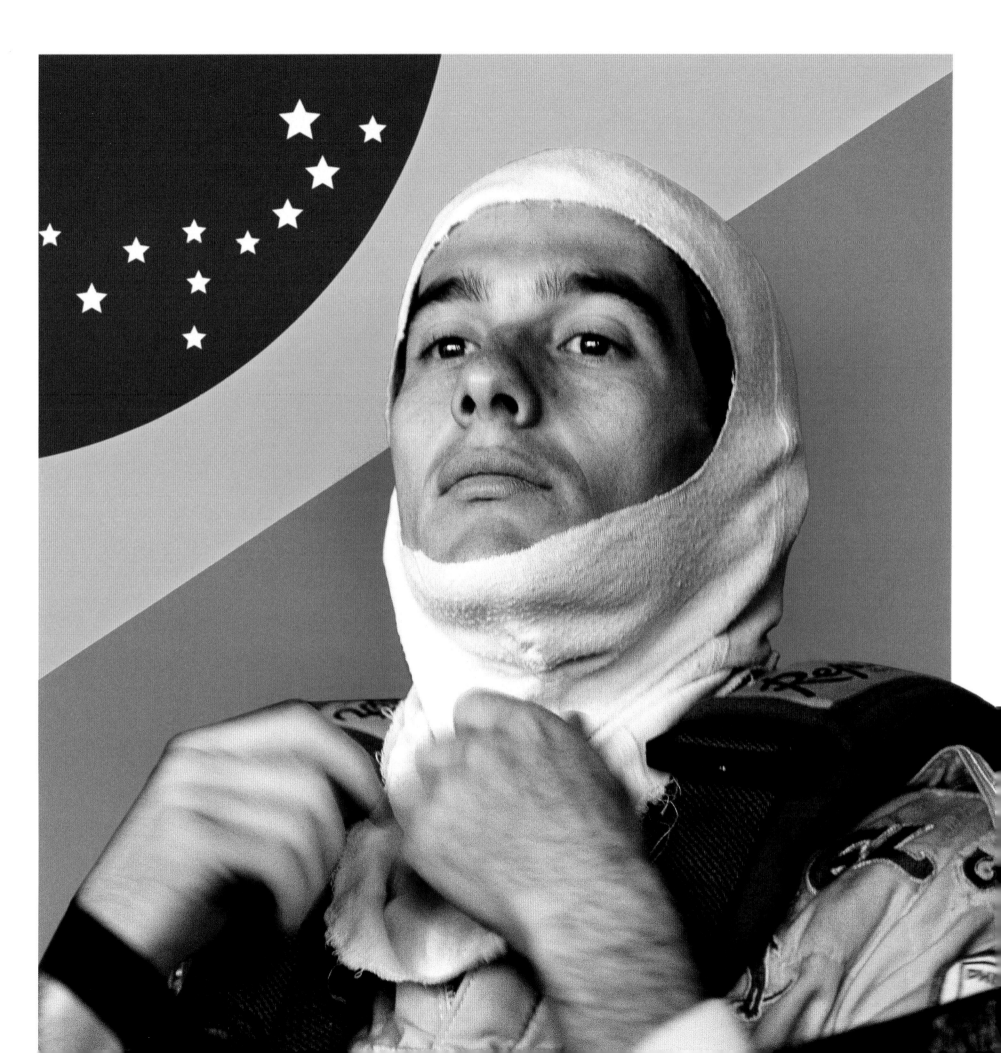

PACESETTERS:
FOUR LOTUS
GRAND PRIX
CARS

LOTUS 25 FLYING BATHTUB

The Lotus 25 made its debut at the Dutch Grand Prix in Zandvoort on 20 May 1962, to the amazement of the media and spectators when its revolutionary monocoque was explained to them – and to the chagrin of the marque's customers who had just bought the space-framed 24 model.

As beautiful as it was efficient – with enormous torsional rigidity and great road-holding – it was to fly the Lotus flag until 1965, followed by its immediate successor in development, the 33, which would grace the race circuits until 1967. The 25 secured 14 grand prix wins in four seasons as well as Jim Clark's and Team Lotus' first titles in 1963, with a yellow stripe running over the front and the rear of the green bodywork.

Colin Chapman's basic idea had been to join two longitudinal fuel tanks by a stressed undertray, two bulkheads fore-and-aft and the instrument panel and then bolt a type 24-like suspension to the front and rear ends. The monocoque was made of aluminium alloy sheet. Quite in keeping with his lightweight philosophy it weighed in at a mere 30 kg. The little car was clad in fibre-glass bodywork and had rubberised fuel bags inside the D-section side pontoons. The man at its tiny steering wheel adopted a hitherto unseen driving position, almost lying down with his seat angled back 35 degrees.

The standard engine/transmission combination was a Coventry Climax V8 joined to a five-speed ZF gearbox. In the dying months of the 1962 season, Lucas injection was introduced, whilst other technical and aerodynamic refinements were also revealed.

LOTUS 49 RACING BEAUTY

On 4 June 1967 another ground-breaking Lotus Formula 1 car made its first appearance in the Dutch seaside resort of Zandvoort: the 49. Its slim and elegant chassis, not designed by Colin Chapman alone, but in collaboration with his talented employee Maurice Phillippe, was to set the benchmark for the early years of the three-litre formula. Although their cars were plagued by teething troubles, Graham Hill secured pole whereas Jim Clark took a convincing victory, almost 24 seconds ahead of runner-up Jack Brabham.

From the Spanish Grand Prix in May 1968 onwards, the 49 and its various metamorphoses, in the striking colour scheme of new sponsor Gold Leaf, would notch up eleven more GP firsts, the last of which, at Monaco in 1970, driven by Jochen Rindt, was arguably its most famous triumph. With his win in the last round of the

1968 season at Mexico City, Graham Hill had clinched the drivers' and constructors' crowns that year.

Part and parcel of the type's success was its brand-new Ford DFV (for double four valves) engine, with 16 valves working in each of the two cylinder banks. This neat and compact 90-degree V8 unit, the creation of Cosworth Engineering's Mike Costin and Keith Duckworth, served as a stressed member. Given to Lotus exclusively in its first year, it produced a little over 400 bhp. Against the wildest of expectations it far exceeded the 49's life span, reaching more than 500 bhp at the end of its amazing career, amassing a total of 155 victories out of 262 races through to 1985.

LOTUS 72 PACE-SETTING WEDGE

The world was growing accustomed to Lotus spearheading progress when, for the 1970 Spanish Grand Prix at Jarama, Colin Chapman's opus 72 was unveiled. The man himself had laid down its lines, whereas Maurice Phillippe had looked after the details. Evolving through to E-specification, the 72 turned out to be the marque's longest-serving front-line racing car design, not least because its successor, the type 76, introduced in 1974, completely failed to live up to expectations. From 1972 in the black and gold colours of the cigarette brand John Player, the 72, with drivers like Jochen Rindt, Emerson Fittipaldi and Ronnie Peterson at the wheel, amassed 20 grand prix wins, three constructors' and two drivers' (for the Austrian and the Brazilian) titles.

Lotus kept faith with the Ford DFV engine which, however, had been sold to the majority of the Formula 1 field since 1968. Innovation prevailed in terms of aerodynamic efficiency, as demonstrated by the 72's dramatic 'shovel' nose and wedge shape, flanked by a couple of mid-mounted radiators.

Other striking features of the car were a rear oil tank for the sake of better weight distribution, inboard-mounted front brakes and torsion bar suspension, later to be replaced by more common solutions. Its weight was very close to the minimum of 530 kg stipulated by motor racing's legislative body, the unsprung weight cut down as well, suiting the 72's symbiosis with the Firestone tyres for which it had been developed.

LOTUS 79
ONE YEAR
WONDER

Competitive for just one season and the perfect tool for Mario Andretti's and Lotus' world championships in 1978, the Type 79 was arguably the epitome of what Colin Chapman called "the unfair example". The 78 of the preceding year, also used for the initial five races in 1978, had been the Hethel outfit's first attempt at a ground-effect car. But the 79 exploited this to the full. Straight out of the box, it was two seconds faster everywhere, securing five wins for Andretti and one for Ronnie Peterson.

The unfair advantage: Ferrari, Lotus' main rival in the seventies, had just pulled three constructors' titles out of the hat. But its wide and low flat-12 engine stood in the way of the Italians developing a true "wing" car with proper venturi tunnels.

Of course, form again followed function. But Chapman's keen eye for aesthetics ensured that this low and sleek machine was also one of the most beautiful racing cars ever made. He controlled the project as a whole, while Lotus engineers Geoff Aldridge and Martin Ogilvie honed the concept into its ultimate shape. Aluminium sheet was used for the monocoque, except for the honeycomb sandwich floor. This was soon reinforced on account of the ground-effect loads. With a single fuel cell inside the tub, the side pods housed only the radiators. The elements of the rear suspension were inboard as well, so that the airflow could pass uninhibited.

In 1979, however, the Red Empire struck back, and Lotus was left nowhere.

HELMSMEN:
TWO LOTUS
LEADERS

COLIN CHAPMAN
RESTLESS
GENIUS

It was a pleasure to talk to Colin Chapman, even if seeing him in Hethel had a touch of an audience about it. What he said was already honed for publication. That made life so much easier for a journalist.

And he had a lot to say. The racing world remembers him hurling his black cap into the air in triumph with an operatic leap whenever one of his cars crossed the finishing line victorious. Even Enzo Ferrari, who dismissed his British rivals as *garagistes,* could not but offer grudging respect. "Chapman was a born leader. What he loved about his team was that he could implement his ideas so quickly – like an Italian *condottiere,*" says Mario Andretti about his former employer. And indeed, recalls legendary Lotus mechanic Bob Dance, his boss needed that quality to motivate his people into slaving away for 73 hours a week on a regular basis. And there was also Chapman the innovator and revolutionary, somebody who always started things off and never copied, as Andretti puts it.

But Peter Warr, Chapman's right-hand man until the Lotus founder's sudden death in 1982 and then team boss for seven more years, tended to tackle that myth. "Aerodynamics had existed long before the Lotus Mk 8. Monocoques had been made before the war. Ground effect wasn't totally new (having already been used for the

Auto Union record cars, for instance). His genius was to be able to take an idea, refine it, adapt it, think it through from a different direction." Chapman himself liked to cultivate the notion of the inventor who received his intuition in the cosy seclusion of his bath-tub or scribbling on a piece of wrapping paper.

But the life of Anthony Colin Bruce Chapman, born in London on 19 May 1928, was also lined with tragedy, some of his finest drivers dying in his fragile and filigree creations. "I've taken blows in my life like nobody else," he brooded. The worst? He would inevitably give a veiled answer to that question: "We all know what can happen in this sport. It's no use always looking for a culprit when that has again been the case." Chapman and Jim Clark had been like kittens in a basket, as former Lotus driver Innes Ireland observed, not without jealousy. Clark's death at Hockenheim in April 1968 inflicted a trauma on him which he was never to get over.

As a young man he used to joke that his retirement age would be 35. He would then put it off in a five-year rhythm. But on 16 December 1982 he succumbed to a heart attack. On the day he died, his latest stroke of genius was track-tested: a car with active suspension.

TONY FERNANDES
HIGH-FLYER

As a boy, Tony Fernandes treasured the model of a Lotus 33, and he used to tell his father that one day he wanted to possess his own Formula 1 team. Not to be a racing driver, mind you, because, to this day, he does not rate his faculties at the wheel too highly.

On 15 September 2009, the FIA announced that Anthony Francis Fernandes, born in Kuala Lumpur in June 1964, did have his own team. And what began as a flirt, seasoned with nostalgia and the clever move to revive the evocative Lotus name rather than calling his squad Fernandes F1 or something similar, has since turned into a veritable love affair. It is the Lotus mystique, as well as the declared aim to bring his native Malaysia right into the heart of Formula 1 and vice versa, that has fully absorbed him. His involvement is motivated by true passion, and often, as was the case during the team's debut at Sepang, you will see Tony Fernandes in tears or freely admitting that he has had a sleepless night or two.

In 2010, however, he had every reason to be a very happy man. In the past eight years, his low-cost airline AirAsia has blossomed under his aegis from humble origins into a smash hit. In that period, his stock of aircraft rose from two to 92, his staff from 250 to 7000, the line's destinations from one to more than 130. AirAsia connects all ten Asian capitals and, thanks to moderate fares, suddenly offers greater mobility and distances to the Asian man in the street. The respected German daily *Süddeutsche Zeitung* recently surmised that Tony's planes do more for integration within the huge continent than all of its politicians.

On 14 April 2010, Tony Fernandes was conferred the title of *Officier de la Légion d'Honneur* by the French government for his outstanding contributions to the aviation industry – the highest rank of honour that can be awarded to a non-French citizen. A fortnight earlier, the affable entrepreneur had been awarded an *Honorary Doctorate of Business Innovation* by the *Universiti Teknologi Malaysia* in Skudai.

These, and his other ongoing activities, such as Tune Hotels and various sports enterprises, often excuse his late arrival in the paddock. For the Classic Team Lotus Festival at Snetterton on 20 June 2010, Tony could only spare one and a half hours before he left for the Silverstone Moto GP in a glaring red helicopter.

His bonds with the Chapman family are warmhearted indeed. At the F1 curtain raiser in Bahrain, Clive Chapman presented a beaming Tony with the legendary black cap his father used to throw in the air each time his team triumphed. This gesture said it all.

APPENDIX

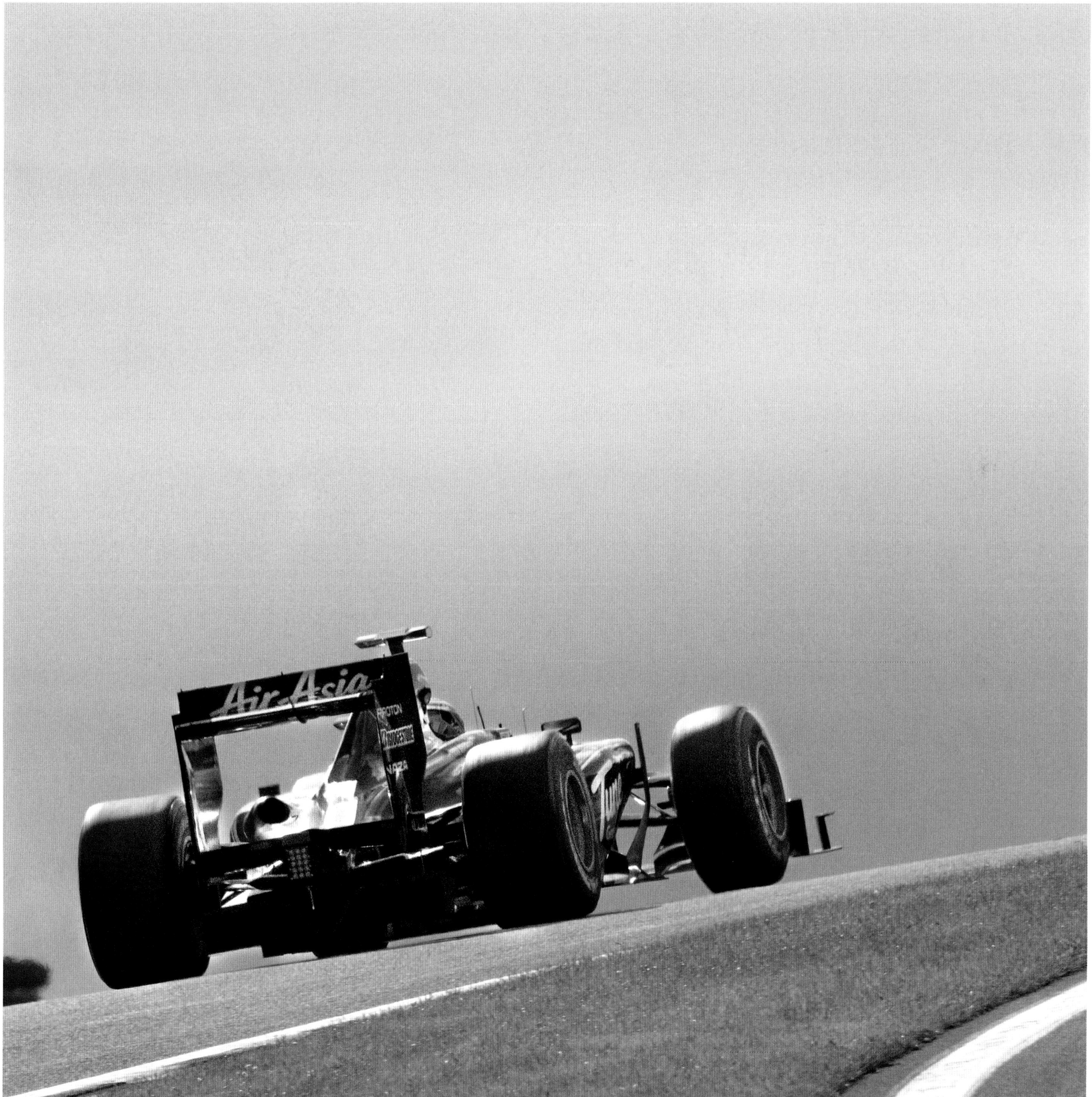
Air Asia

ALWAYS ONE STEP AHEAD: LOTUS AND FORMULA 1

On 15 September 2009, the FIA (Fédération Internationale de l'Automobile) announced the return of Lotus to Formula 1.

Those two syllables, blending euphony and a touch of exotic mystery, opened the doors to a myth. Still fourth in the all-time grand prix rankings from 1950 to the present day, claiming six drivers' championships and seven constructors' titles, the team gleaned 79 race victories and 107 pole positions from 491 starts. With a touch of patriotic enthusiasm, the renowned motor racing publication *Motor Sport* christened the marque "England's Ferrari". But whilst the leading triumvirate of Italy's Ferrari, McLaren and Williams diligently continued collecting points and positions for eternity, Lotus fell into 15 years of Sleeping Beauty slumbers.

Without actually tarnishing the Lotus legend retrospectively, the end had been a sad affair. Money was tight and the energetic founding father was gone. The premature death of indefatigable innovator Anthony Colin Bruce Chapman, his ACBC initials interwoven in the Lotus badge, left a vacuum. Peter Warr, Chapman's team manager and successor, presided over a brief resurgence between 1985 and 1987, largely thanks to Ayrton Senna, the up-and-coming Brazilian wunderkind.

Creative, impatient and choleric, Colin Chapman (1928-1982) was not the easiest of bosses. Known as "Mr. Lotus", he was synonymous with his creations. He drew his inspiration, he declared, from the cloistered seclusion of his bathtub or by scribbling on a scrap of toilet paper or packaging, his hand guided by the muse. Nevertheless, he was not an inventor in the classical sense. Rather, as Peter Warr noted, Colin latched onto existing ideas and maximized their potential. For his part, Chapman had to look on as others pounced on his concepts, refined them and beat him at his own game. In many ways, the McLaren M23 designed by Gordon Coppuck in 1973 was a sublimated bootleg of the Lotus 72. And Chapman's Type 78 and 79 "wing" cars

inspired racetrack rivals, Ligier and Williams, to come up with vehicles which were markedly superior to the originals. Chapman was a forceful character whose style it was to thrash out an idea and point it in the right direction – leaving the precision work to his employees.

The motor racing fraternity remembers his recurring gesture of triumph. After each GP victory for his marque he would perform a theatrical lunge on the home straight and fling his black cap to the skies. The last such cameo was in 1982 at the Österreichring, when Rome's handsome Elio de Angelis snatched victory from Williams driver Keke Rosberg by a matter of inches. Chapman already joked about retiring at the young age of 35, subsequently pushing back his self-appointed pension age every five years. A heart attack on 16 December 1982 relieved him of the decision once and for all. It struck him down just as he was designing a vehicle with active suspension. The deaths of Lotus drivers such as Mike Spence, Jochen Rindt and Ronnie Peterson had taken their toll on him, none more so that that of his alter ego Jim Clark in April 1968, at a non-championship Formula 2 race in Hockenheim.

Chapman was a forward thinker, giving progress a name in the serial numbers of his creations, a Köchel catalogue of a technical genius. The Lotus 25 of 1963 – as minimalist as it was beautiful – was the first F1 racing car to enter the fray with a monocoque. The design was based on an underbody which connected two petrol tanks, mounted lengthways, with two sturdy transverse bulkheads and the instrument panel. The man at the steering wheel almost had to lie down in this aluminium tub. The concept garnered 14 grand prix victories in four seasons, along with the first championships for Clark and Team Lotus in 1963. Two years later, the car's direct descendant, the Lotus 33, proved a similar success.

The unique Type 38 was rather a footnote, a one-off designed with the specific aim of winning the Indianapolis 500 in 1965. Comparatively tiny, yet commanding, it got the job done on foreign soil with the swift Scotsman at the helm.

The next milestone which cemented Chapman's place in Formula 1 history was the Lotus 49 of 1967, which made its first appearance at the Dutch Grand Prix in June of that year. Screaming down the neck of the winner Jim Clark was a Ford DFV engine, freshly developed by its spiritual fathers Mike Costin and Keith Duckworth. This compact V8 with 32 valves would notch up an impressive 155 victories until 1985. It was already integrated into the Type 49 as an element of the load-bearing structure.

Chapman pulled another ace from his sleeve, of a more commercial nature, the following year. Starting with the Spanish GP of 1968, his racing fleet rolled up to the starting grid in the red, white and gold livery of the Gold Leaf sponsor. The whiskered

Brit had prepared the coup in the Tasman Series and Formula 2. In the space age, he suggested, motor racing also required more sophisticated technology. Moreover, the introduction of the three-litre formula in 1966 had made the top tier of racing a much more expensive affair. External sources, such as cigarette manufacturers, were there to be tapped into – still an established practice today.

The Type 49 delivered eleven victories, the last at Monaco in 1970, where Jochen Rindt's impetuous attacks irritated Jack Brabham to such an extent that the veteran pilot left the track on the final bend of the final lap and headed into bales of straw. The Type 72, another pioneering Lotus construction, followed hot on the heels of its predecessor, albeit with a few early teething troubles. The 72 would prove to be the marque's longest serving open wheel car out in front. From 1972 onwards, in the black and gold of the sponsor, John Player, and with drivers like Jochen Rindt, Emerson Fittipaldi and Ronnie Peterson at the wheel, it amassed 20 GP triumphs, three constructors' titles and the two drivers' championships for the Austrian and the Brazilian. Had their formidable brace of drivers, Fittipaldi and Peterson, not taken points off each other in 1973, the score would have been even higher. Lotus kept faith with the Ford DFV engine which had had been sold to the majority of Formula 1 constructors since 1968. Innovation reigned in terms of aerodynamic efficiency. This was achieved by the 72's sharply tapered nose and the wedge-shaped monocoque, flanked by two side mounted radiators.

The perfect instrument for the double championships of Lotus and Mario Andretti in 1978, the Type 79 dominated the world of Formula 1 for just a single season. It was perhaps the most conspicuous manifestation of Chapman's beloved "unfair advantage", as he called it. He was referring to the moulding of the chassis as a "wing" car, which literally clung to the road surface. The previous year's Type 78, also deployed in the first five races of the 1978 grand prix cycle, represented a first step in this direction. The Type 79 exploited the principle to the full, perhaps becoming the most attractive racing car of the decade in the process. Nevertheless, the red Ferrari empire struck back in 1979, with Lotus finishing nowhere.

The common multiple of the five world champions Clark (1963 and 1965), Hill (1968), Rindt (1970), Fittipaldi (1972) and Andretti (1978), along with other F1 greats who served the team, like Moss, Peterson and Senna, can be traced back to the simple fact that they drove for Lotus. Indeed, they could barely have been a more diverse group of individuals. First, there was Stirling Moss, who worked miracles at the wheel of the blue and white Lotus 18 and 18/21 for Rob Walker's private racing team. Then there was Jim Clark, almost symbiotically linked to Chapman. Both incredibly fast and extremely shy, the proud Scot was deeply committed to his homeland. Torn between the cockpit and a shepherd's crook is how the media portrayed him, and they were not so far off the mark. Then there was Graham Hill, the "moustachioed Londoner", as they called him. A legend in his own lifetime, he fell victim to a tragic plane crash in late November 1975, having only recently hung up his black helmet with the vertical white stripes, his rowing club's colours.

The swashbuckling Austrian Jochen Rindt, the "King of Formula 2", as he was known, was also a Formula 1 sovereign in 1970. That he was awarded that dignity posthumously after his fatal crash in Monza is one of the sport's great absurdities. There was the young, brilliantly talented Emerson Fittipaldi, heralding a veritable tradition of Brazilian champions. Then there was the fair-haired Swede Ronnie Peterson. Beneath his cool and calm exterior, "SuperSwede" was a spectacular, daring driver like Rindt before him and Gilles Villeneuve after him. The American Mario Andretti, at once jovial and gruff, could have accomplished so much more on the grand prix scene, had it not been for his own legendary versatility. And of course the great Ayrton Senna, who embarked on a career of superlatives by procuring six of his 41 grand prix victories whilst driving for the Hethel make. The insignia of the glorious Team Lotus had well and truly earned its place in the history books by this point.

It was the dynamic entrepreneur Tony Fernandes from Kuala Lumpur who brought the myth back to life. His Lotus Racing ensemble, bearing the time-honoured green and yellow livery, is an Anglo-Malaysian joint venture which transcends the borders of the Global Village. His gleaming racers, the T127s, in customary Lotus numerical fashion, arrived right on schedule for the 2010 season at the first practice session in sun-drenched Bahrain. Before the race, Clive Chapman, son of the late Colin Chapman, presented Fernandes with his father's black cap. The message attached read: "For when next needed" – for the next victory.

In its maiden year the outfit impressively manifested its superiority among the F1 newcomers. There is more at stake in 2011, with Tony's squad sporting the magic Team Lotus logo again. The saga has come full circle.

SENTIASA SELANGKAH DI HADAPAN: LOTUS DAN FORMULA 1

Pada 15 September 2009, FIA (Fédération Internationale de l'Automobile) mengumumkan kekembalian Lotus kepada Formula 1.

Dua suku kata unik yang hebat lagi eksotik yang membuka pintu ke sebuah mitos. Masih di tempat keempat pada kedudukan sepanjang masa Grand Prix dari tahun 1950 sehinggalah ke hari ini, meraih enam kejohanan pemandu dan tujuh kemenangan pembina, pasukan ini memungut 79 kejuaraan perlumbaan dan 107 kedudukan terdepan daripada 491 permulaan. Dengan sentuhan semangat patriotisme, terbitan perlumbaan motor yang terkemuka, *Motor Sport*, memberi pasukan ini nama "England's Ferrari". Namun sementara jaguh bertiga Itali yang terunggul, iaitu Ferrari, McLaren dan Williams, dengan tekunnya terus memungut mata dan kedudukan yang abadi, Lotus seolah-olah terlena selama 16 tahun.

Tanpa niat mencemarkan legenda Lotus secara retrospektif, kesudahannya amat menyedihkan. Hal ehwal kewangannya berkeadaan suram dan bapa pengasas yang penuh bertenaga sudah tiada lagi. Kematian penginovasi gigih, Anthony Colin Bruce Chapman yang mengejutkan, singkatan huruf namanya, ACBC, tersulam pada lambang Lotus, meninggalkan suatu kekosongan. Peter Warr, pengurus pasukan dan pengganti Chapman, menjadi ketua semasa kebangkitan semulanya yang singkat antara tahun 1985 hingga 1987, terutamanya disebabkan Ayrton Senna yang termasyhur dari Brazil.

Colin Chapman (1928-1982) yang kreatif, tidak penyabar dan pemarah bukanlah ketua yang paling mudah berpuas hati. Beliau digelar "Mr. Lotus" dan disinonimkan dengan ciptaannya. Beliau mendapat inspirasi, kata beliau, apabila keseorangan di dalam tab mandinya, ataupun dengan mencoret pada secebis tisu tandas atau kertas bungkusan, tangannya berpandukan ilhamnya. Namun demikian, beliau bukanlah pereka cipta dalam erti kata yang lazim. Sebaliknya, seperti yang diperhatikan oleh Peter Warr, Colin menggunakan idea yang sedia ada dan memanfaatkan potensi idea itu sepenuhnya. Chapman terpaksa memandang sahaja apabila orang lain mengambil konsepnya, memperbaik konsep itu dan mengatasinya dalam permainannya sendiri. McLaren M23 yang direka bentuk oleh Gordon Coppuck pada tahun 1973 merupakan anak haram Lotus 72. Dan *Wing Cars* Jenis 78 dan 79 oleh Chapman telah memberi inspirasi kepada pesaing litar lumba dekad 1970-an, iaitu Ligier dan Williams, untuk menghasilkan kenderaan yang dengan ketaranya lebih bagus daripada yang asal. Chapman yang bersifat tegas dan bersemangat, gemar melemparkan sesuatu idea dan menukar haluannya ke arah yang betul, dan membiarkan para pekerjanya melakukan kerja-kerja rumit.

Industri perlumbaan motor masih ingat lagaknya sebagai juara apabila beliau memberi penghormatan kepada dirinya sendiri dengan tepuk sanjungan sambil berdiri. Selepas setiap kemenangan GP bagi jenamanya, beliau akan melakukan lagak terpaan penuh drama dan melemparkan topi hitamnya ke udara. Kali yang terakhir ialah pada tahun 1982 di Österreichring, apabila Elio de Angelis yang kacak dari Rome merampas kemenangan daripada pemandu Williams, Keke Rosberg, mendahului sebanyak beberapa inci sahaja. Chapman sudah pun bergurau tentang hasratnya untuk bersara pada usia muda 35 tahun, seterusnya melambatkan pula usia persaraannya ini setiap lima tahun. Serangan jantung pada 16 Disember 1982 membuat keputusan ini untuknya. Penyakit ini menyerang ketika beliau mereka bentuk kenderaan dengan suspensi aktif. Kematian pemandu seperti Mike Spence, Jochen Rindt dan Ronnie Peterson besar kesannya terhadap beliau, begitu juga dengan kematian Jim Clark pada bulan April 1968, semasa perlumbaan Formula 2 yang tidak berapa penting di Hockenheim.

Chapman sentiasa berfikiran ke depan. Beliau memberi nama kepada kemajuan dalam bentuk nombor bersiri pada ciptaannya, sebuah katalog Köchel kepunyaan seorang yang berbakat teknikal. Lotus 25 pada tahun 1963, seringkas keindahannya, ialah kereta lumba F1 yang pertama sekali bertanding dengan monocoque. Reka bentuknya didasarkan pada dasar badan yang menyambungkan dua tangki petrol, dipasang secara memanjang dan dilengkapi dua dinding sekat melintang yang kukuh, dan panel alat. Pemandunya, Jim Clark, hampir-hampir berbaring di dalam badan aluminiumnya. Konsep ini berjaya memperoleh 14 kemenangan Grand Prix di dalam empat musim, berserta kejuaraan yang pertama bagi Clark dan Team Lotus 1963. Dua tahun kemudian, pewaris kereta ini, Lotus 33, mencapai kejayaan yang serupa.

Jenis 38 yang unik ini layak diberi nota kakinya sendiri, direka bentuk dengan tujuan khusus, iaitu untuk memenangi perlumbaan Indianapolis 500 pada tahun 1965. Kereta yang secara bandingannya kecil tetapi nyata ini memenuhi matlamatnya di atas tanah asing dengan pemandu dari Scotland.

Batu penanda yang seterusnya, yang telah menempa tempat Chapman dalam sejarah Formula 1 ialah Lotus 49 pada tahun 1967, yang pertama kali muncul semasa

Grand Prix Belanda pada tahun Jun tahun itu. Pemenangnya, Jim Clark, memandu kereta berenjin Ford DFV, yang baru sahaja dihasilkan oleh Mike Costin dan Keith Duckworth. Enjin V8 yang padat dengan 32 injap ini berjaya meraih 155 kemenangan sehingga tahun 1985. Sudah disepadukan dengan Jenis 49 sebagai unsur binaan penampung beban.

Chapman sekali lagi menunjukkan kehandalannya dengan cara yang lebih komersial pada tahun yang berikutnya. Bermula dengan GP Sepanyol pada tahun 1968, kumpulan kereta lumbanya beredar ke grid pemula dengan warna pengenal merah, putih dan emas penajanya, iaitu Gold Leaf. Warga Britain yang bermisai ini sudah pun bersiap sedia semasa Siri Tasman dan Formula 2. Pada zaman angkasa, katanya, perlumbaan motor juga memerlukan teknologi yang lebih canggih. Lagipun, pengenalan rumusan 3 liter telah menjadikan peringkat perlumbaan yang tertinggi ini jauh lebih mahal. Sumber luaran, seperti pengilang rokok, boleh dipergunakan pada ketika itu, dan masih dipergunakan hari ini.

Jenis 49 mencapai sebelas kemenangan, yang terakhir di Monaco pada tahun 1970, apabila serangan Jochen Rindt yang terburu-buru menimbulkan rasa begitu geram pada Jack Brabham sehinggakan pemandu veteran tersebut meninggalkan litar di selekoh yang terakhir dan merempuh bandela-bandela jerami. Jenis 72, suatu lagi binaan Lotus, mengikuti rapat di belakang pendahulunya, tetapi mengalami beberapa masalah awal. Jenis 72 ini akhirnya menjadi kereta roda terbuka jenama ini yang paling lama berkhidmat. Mulai tahun 1972, dengan warna pengenal hitam dan emas penajanya, iaitu John Player, dan dengan pemandu seperti Jochen Rindt, Emerson Fittipaldi dan Ronnie Peterson, kereta ini meraih 20 kejohanan GP, tiga kemenangan pembina dan dua kejuaraan pemandu bagi anak Austria dan Brazil ini. Jika para pemandunya yang mengagumkan, Fittipaldi and Peterson, tidak menolak mata daripada satu sama lain pada tahun 1973, mata akhirnya pasti lebih tinggi lagi. Lotus tetap menaruh kepercayaannya terhadap enjin Ford DFV yang telah dijual kepada kebanyakan pembina Formula 1 sejak tahun 1968. Inovasinya ketara dari segi kecekapan aerodinamik. Ini dicapai dengan muncung yang runcing pada Jenis 72 ini, dengan ruang pemandu berbentuk baji yang dilengkapi penyinar sisi pada kiri kanannya.

Jenis 79 ialah alat yang sempurna untuk kejuaraan kembar Lotus dan Marion Andretti pada tahun 1978, dan telah menguasai dunia Formula 1 selama satu musim sahaja. Ini mungkin tanda yang paling nyata tentang "kelebihan yang tidak adil" kesayangan Chapman, iaitu gelaran yang diberikannya sendiri. Beliau merujuk kepada kumai casisnya sebagai *Wing Car*, yang mampu melekap pada permukaan jalan. Jenis 78 pada tahun sebelumnya, juga digunakan semasa lima perlumbaan pertama di dalam kitaran Grand Prix tahun 1978, merupakan pembuka langkah ke arah ini. Jenis 79 memanfaatkan prinsip ini sepenuhnya, mungkin menjadi kereta lumba yang paling

menarik pada dekad ini dalam proses tersebut. Namun demikian, empayar merah Ferrari kembali lagi pada tahun 1979, dengan Lotus tidak mendapat tempat.

Juara sedunia berlima, iaitu Clark (1963 dan 1965), Hill (1968), Rindt (1970), Fittipaldi (1972) dan Andretti (1978), bersama-sama dengan anggota F1 yang lain di dalam pasukan ini, seperti Peterson dan Senna, boleh dikesan balik kepada hakikat bahawa mereka memandu untuk Lotus. Sememangnya, merekalah kumpulan yang paling pelbagai. Seterusnya ialah Stirling Moss yang sungguh handal memandu Lotus 18 dan Lotus 18/21 yang berwarna biru dan putih untuk pasukan lumba persendirian Rob Walker. Pertama, terkait dengan Chapman dengan cara yang seolah-olah simbiotik, Jim Clark amat pantas tetapi juga amat pemalu orangnya, rakyat Scotland yang komited secara mendalam terhadap tanah airnya. Pihak media menggambarkannya sebagai berada antara ruang pemandu dengan tongkat gembala lembu, dan gambaran mereka agak tepat. Seterusnya ialah Graham Hill, "warga London yang bermisai". Legenda ini menjadi mangsa kapal terbang yang terhempas pada lewat bulan November 1975, setelah baru sahaja menyimpan topi keledarnya yang berwarna hitam berbelang putih, iaitu warna pengenal kelab perahunya.

Jochen Rindt yang ranggi dari Australia, "Raja Formula 2", juga raja Formula 1 pada tahun 1970, gelaran yang secara tidak munasabahnya diperoleh walaupun selepas terbunuh dalam kemalangan di Monza. Emerson Fittipaldi yang muda dan sungguh berbakat pula meneruskan tradisi juara dari Brazil. Di sebalik penampilan tenang Ronnie Peterson dari Sweden, "SuperSwede" ini sebenarnya pemandu yang ghairah dan berani seperti Rindt sebelumnya dan Gilles Villeneuve selepasnya. Mario Andretti dari Amerika bersifat riang tetapi kasar, mampu mencapai jauh lebih banyak di arena Grand Prix jika tidak kerana sifatnya yang serba boleh. Dan sudah tentu sekali Ayrton Senna yang agung, yang memulakan kerjaya penuh keamatan dengan memperoleh enam daripada 41 kemenangan Grand Prix miliknya semasa memandu untuk jenama Lotus. Tanda kebesaran Team Lotus telah mendapat tempatnya di dalam buku sejarah dengan hakikat ini.

Usahawan Tony Fernandes yang dinamik dari Kuala Lumpur telah menghidupkan kembali mitos ini. Pakaian Lotus Racing berwarna hijau dan kuning yang dikenakannya boleh dipandang sebagai usaha sama Inggeris-Malaysia yang melintasi sempadan *Global Village*. Pelumbanya, T127, dengan gaya Lotus yang bernombor, tiba tepat pada masanya untuk menghadiri sesi latihan yang pertama pada musim 2010 di Bahrain. Sebelum perlumbaan bermula, Clive Chapman, anak lelaki mendiang Colin Chapman, menghadiahkan topi hitam bapanya kepada Fernandes. Mesej yang tertulis padanya ialah: "Apabila diperlukan kelak" – untuk kemenangan yang seterusnya. Pada tahunnya yang pertama, kumpulan ini menonjolkan keagungannya dalam kalangan pendatang baharu ke F1. Lebih banyak yang dipertaruhkan pada tahun 2011, dengan skuad Tony membawa logo Team Lotus yang ajaib itu sekal lagi. Kini lengkaplah kitaran saga ini.

IMMER EINEN SCHRITT VORAUS: LOTUS UND DIE FORMEL 1

Am 15. September 2009 verkündete die FIA (Fédération Internationale de l'Automobile), Lotus werde in die Formel 1 zurückkehren.

Die beiden Silben, in denen sich auf eigentümliche Weise Wohlklang und Exotik zusammenfinden, stießen die Tür zu einem Mythos auf. Noch immer hält die Marke auf der ewigen Bestenliste der Grands Prix seit 1950 den vierten Rang, mit sechs Fahrer- und sieben Konstrukteurstiteln sowie 79 Siegen und 107 Pole-Positions als Ausbeute aus 491 Starts. „Englands Ferrari" nannte sie die angesehene und vaterländisch gesonnene Fachpublikation *Motor Sport* kürzlich. Aber während die drei Führenden, Italiens Ferrari, McLaren und Williams, noch immer emsig Positionen und Punkte für die Unsterblichkeit sammelten, versank Lotus 16 lange Jahre in einem Dornröschenschlaf.

Schon das Ende war trist gewesen, ohne indessen aus der Rückschau die Lotus-Legende nachhaltig zu beschädigen. Das Geld fehlte und natürlich der umtriebige Gründervater, Motor und rastlose Neuerer, dessen Initialen ACBC (für Anthony Colin Bruce Chapman) sich im Lotus-Emblem ineinander verschlingen. Nach seinem vorzeitigen Tod gab es unter seinem Teamchef und Nachfolger Peter Warr noch einmal eine kurze Blüte zwischen 1985 und '87, vor allem dank Ayrton Senna, dem aufstrebenden brasilianischen Wunderknaben.

Colin Chapman (1928–1982): kreativ, ungeduldig, cholerisch, kein einfacher Chef. Sie identifizierten ihn mit seinen Produkten und nannten ihn „Mr. Lotus". Seine Inspiration, erklärte er sich selbst, beziehe er in der Abgeschiedenheit und Klausur seiner Badewanne oder auf einem Stück Pack- oder Klopapier kritzelnd, während ihm die Muse gewissermaßen die Hand führe. Dennoch kein Erfinder im klassischen Sinn: „Colin", sagte Peter Warr über ihn, „griff eigentlich bereits bestehende Ideen auf und machte dann das Beste aus ihnen." Seinerseits musste Chapman zuschauen,

wie sich andere über seine Konzepte hermachten, sie verfeinerten und ihn dann damit schlugen. Bei dem Typ M23 des McLaren-Designers Gordon Coppuck anno 1973 handelte es sich um eine sublimierte Raubkopie des Lotus 72. Und Chapmans „Wing Cars" Typ 78 und 79 inspirierten Ende der siebziger Jahren die Rivalen auf der Rennbahn Ligier und Williams zu Fahrzeugen, die den Originalen eindeutig überlegen waren. Überhaupt war Chapman der Mann fürs Grobe im besten Sinne – er gab die Marschlinie vor und überließ die Feinarbeit seinen Mitarbeitern.

Die Branche erinnert sich seiner in einer wiederkehrenden Triumphgebärde und stehenden Ovation an sich selbst. Nach jedem GP-Erfolg der Marke grätschte er in einem opernhaften Ausfallschritt auf die Zielgerade und schleuderte seine schwarze Kappe in den Himmel. Dies geschah zum letzten Mal, als sich der schöne Römer Elio de Angelis 1982 auf dem Österreichring den Sieg eine Handbreit vor Williams-Mann Keke Rosberg schnappte. Schon mit 35, scherzte der junge Chapman, werde er sich in den Ruhestand zurückziehen, und schob anschließend das selbst gewählte Pensionsalter in einem Fünf-Jahres-Rhythmus vor sich her. Am 16. Dezember 1982 nahm ihm ein Herzinfarkt die Enscheidung für immer ab. Er erwischte ihn mitten in der Planung für ein Fahrzeug mit aktiver Aufhängung. Der Tod seiner Fahrer wie Mike Spence, Jochen Rindt und Ronnie Peterson hatte ihn schwer belastet, vor allem aber der von Jim Clark im April 1968 in einem unbedeutenden Formel-2-Rennen in Hockenheim.

Chapman der Vordenker: Der Fortschritt hatte immer einen Namen in der fortlaufenden Nummerierung seiner Werke – Köchelverzeichnis eines technischen Genies. Der Lotus 25 von 1963 – ebenso minimalistisch wie schön – wartete als erster F1-Rennwagen mit einem Monocoque auf. Der Gedanke dahinter: zwei längsgerichtete Benzintanks mittels eines tragenden Unterbodens, zweier kräftiger Querschotts und der Armaturentafel miteinander zu verbinden. Der Mann am Lenkrad, allen voran Jim Clark, nahm in dieser Aluminium-Wanne eine fast liegende Haltung ein. Das Konzept reichte zu 14 Grand-Prix-Siegen in vier Saisons sowie den ersten Kronen für Clark und Team Lotus 1963. Zwei Jahre später folgte der direkte Abkömmling Lotus 33, kaum weniger erfolgreich.

Nur eine Fußnote blieb das Unikat Typ 38, hergestellt mit dem einzigen Ziel, die 500 Meilen von Indianapolis 1965 zu gewinnen. Dies tat er auch, vergleichsweise winzig, aber souverän, auf fremdem Terrain, mit dem schnellen Schotten am Volant.

Der nächste Meilenstein, den Chapman in die Geschichte der Formel 1 einpflanzte, war der Lotus 49 von 1967, der beim Großen Preis von Holland im Juni jenes Jahres seine Aufwartung machte. Im Nacken des Siegers Jim Clark brüllte der just von seinen geistigen Vätern Mike Costin und Keith Duckworth geschaffene Ford DFV-Motor. Das war ein kompakter V8 mit 32 Ventilen, auf dessen Konto bis 1985 stattliche 155 Erfolge gehen sollten. Im Typ 49 wurde er bereits als Element der tragenden Struktur eingesetzt.

Ein weiteres Ass, diesmal kommerzieller Natur, zog Chapman ein Jahr später aus dem Ärmel. Vom GP von Spanien 1968 an rollte sein rasender Fuhrpark in den rotweißgoldenen Farben des Geldgebers Gold Leaf an den Start. Diesen Coup hatte der schnurrbärtige Brite in der Tasman-Serie und in der Formel 2 vorbereitet. Im Zeitalter der Raumfahrt, begründete er das, bedürfe es auch im Rennsport ausgeklügelter Technik. Überdies habe sich dessen Königsklasse mit der Einführung der Dreiliter-Formel 1966 beträchtlich verteuert. Da müsse man halt externe Quellen wie so einen Zigaretten-Hersteller anzapfen – ein etabliertes Verfahren bis zum heutigen Tag.

Elf Siege lieferte der Typ 49 ab, den letzten 1970 in Monaco unter Jochen Rindt, vor dessen ungestümen Attacken sich der altgediente Fuhrmann Jack Brabham noch in der letzten Kurve der letzten Runde in die Strohballen verirrte. Da war eigentlich schon der Typ 72 aktuell, eine weitere bahnbrechende Lotus-Kreation, gleichwohl ursprünglich von Kinderkrankheiten heimgesucht. Der 72 erwies sich als der am längsten eingesetzte Monoposto der Marke in Führungsposition. Er häufte, ab 1972 im Schwarzgold des Sponsors John Player, mit Fahrern wie Jochen Rindt, Emerson Fittipaldi und Ronnie Peterson am Lenkrad, bis 1975 20 GP-Triumphe, drei Konstrukteurs- und die beiden Fahrer-Meisterschaften für den Österreicher und den Brasilianer an. Es wären noch mehr gewesen, hätte nicht die starke Fahrer-Riege Fittipaldi und Peterson 1973 einander die Punkte weggenommen. Lotus hatte dem Ford DFV die Treue gehalten, der seit 1968 an die Mehrheit der F1-Hersteller verkauft wurde. Innovation herrschte in punkto aerodynamische Effizienz. Diese wurde erzeugt durch die spitz zulaufende Schaufel-Nase des 72 und den Keil, den seine Fahrgastzelle bildete, flankiert von zwei mittschiffs angebrachten Kühlern.

Nur für eine Saison beherrschte der Typ 79 die Formel-1-Welt, das perfekte Werkzeug für die beiden Championate, die Lotus und Mario Andretti 1978 verbuchten. In ihm hatte vielleicht am auffälligsten Gestalt angenommen, was Chapman „the unfair advantage" nannte und liebte. Der ungerechte Vorteil bestand in der Ausformung des Chassis als „Wing Car", das sich förmlich am Boden festlutschte. Das Modell 78 im Jahr zuvor und bei den ersten fünf Läufen des Grand-Prix-Zyklus 1978 war der erste Ansatz in dieser Richtung gewesen. Der Typ 79 nutzte das Prinzip voll aus und geriet dabei wohl zum attraktivsten Rennwagen des Jahrzehnts. 1979 schlug gleichwohl das rote Imperium Ferrari zurück, und die Lotus landeten im Nirgendwo.

Das gemeinsame Vielfache der fünf Weltmeister Clark (1963 und 1965), Hill (1968), Rindt (1970), Fittipaldi (1972) und Andretti (1978) sowie anderer F1-Granden im Dienste der Marke wie Moss, Peterson und Senna bestand im Wesentlichen darin, dass

sie Lotus fuhren. Denn noch unterschiedlicher können Männer gar nicht sein. Da war Stirling Moss, der am Lenkrad der blauweißen Lotus 18 und 18/21 des privaten Rennstallbesitzers Rob Walker wahre Wunder wirkte. Da war Jim Clark, mit Chapman fast schon bis hin zur Symbiose verbandelt, jenseits von schnell, dabei zutiefst scheu und seiner schottischen Herkunft und Heimat innig verpflichtet. Hin- und hergezogen zwischen Hirtenstab und Cockpit, so sahen ihn die Medien, und da war wohl auch was Wahres dran. Da war der „schnauzbärtige Londoner" Graham Hill, schon zu Lebzeiten ein Denkmal seiner selbst bis zu seinem tragischen Flugzeugabsturz Ende November 1975. Er hatte seinen schwarzen Sturzhelm mit den senkrechten weißen Farbbalken, den Farben seines Ruderclubs, just an den Nagel gehängt.

Da war der verwegene Österreicher Jochen Rindt, der „König der Formel 2", wie sie ihn nannten, 1970 auch ein Souverän der Formel 1 – nach und trotz seinem Unfalltod in Monza, eine der Absurditäten, die dieser Sport bereithält. Da war das junge, strahlende Talent Emerson Fittipaldi, der eine förmliche Tradition brasilianischer Champions einläutete. Da war der blonde Schwede Ronnie Peterson („SuperSwede"), äußerlich ruhig und gelassen, aber ein Vulkan am Volant und Draufgänger wie vor ihm Rindt und nach ihm Gilles Villeneuve. Da war der jovial-bärbeißige Amerikaner Mario Andretti, dem nur seine legendäre Vielseitigkeit dabei im Wege stand, in der Grand-Prix-Sparte noch viel mehr abzuräumen. Und da war der große Ayrton Senna, der sich selbst und der Marke Lotus am Beginn einer Karriere der Superlative mit sechs seiner insgesamt 41 Grand-Prix-Siege beschenkte. Da stand die Schrift für das glorreiche Team Lotus bereits an der Wand.

Wach geküsst wurde der Mythos durch den dynamischen Unternehmer Tony Fernandes aus Kuala Lumpur. Sein Aufgebot Lotus Racing trug das traditionelle Farbschema aus Grün und Gelb, verstand sich aber als anglo-malaysisches Joint Venture jenseits der Zäune des Global Village. Seine blitzsauberen Renner, in überkommener Lotus-Zählung T127 geheißen, erschienen pünktlich zur ersten Trainingssitzung beim Saisonauftakt 2010 im sonnendurchglühten Bahrain. Vor dem Rennen schenkte ihm Clive Chapman, Sohn des verstorbenen Colin Chapman, die berühmte schwarze Kappe seines Vaters. Auf dem begleitenden Zettel stand „For when next needed" – für den nächsten Sieg. Im Debütjahr behauptete man sich eindrucksvoll als Klassenbester unter den Neuankömmlingen in der Formel 1. 2011 ist viel mehr im Visier. Der Rennstall wird wieder Team Lotus heißen. Der Kreis hat sich geschlossen.

SIEMPRE LLEVANDO LA DELANTERA: LOTUS Y LA FÓRMULA 1

El 15 de septiembre de 2009 la FIA (Fédération Internationale de l'Automobile) informó de que Lotus iba a volver a la Fórmula 1.

Las dos sílabas, en las que se reúnen inconfundiblemente la armonía y el exotismo, abrieron la puerta a un mito. La marca ocupa desde 1950 el cuarto lugar en la eterna lista de los mejores Grandes Premios, con seis Campeonatos de Pilotos y siete de Constructores, además de 79 victorias y 107 pole positions obtenidos gracias a 491 primeras posiciones. Hace poco *Motor Sport*, publicación alemana del gremio que goza de gran renombre y tiene un cierto tinte patriótico, llamó a Lotus "el Ferrari de Inglaterra". Pero mientras las tres grandes marcas de la Fórmula 1 (Ferrari italiano, McLaren y Williams) recolectaban diligentemente puntos y posiciones para la inmortalidad, Lotus se hundió durante 16 largos años en un profundo sueño.

Fue un final triste, sin que por ello quedara dañada retrospectivamente y de forma duradera la leyenda Lotus. Faltaban el dinero y el laborioso fundador de la marca, su motor e infatigable innovador, cuyas iniciales ACBC (Anthony Colin Bruce Chapman) se abrazan en el emblema de Lotus. Tras la muerte prematura de Chapman, y a las órdenes de su jefe de equipo y sucesor Peter Warr, la marca experimentó un breve momento de auge entre 1985 y 1987, especialmente gracias a Ayrton Senna, el floreciente prodigio brasileño.

Colin Chapman (1928-1982) no fue un jefe nada fácil, era creativo, impaciente y colérico. Se le identificaba con sus productos y le llamaban "Mr. Lotus". Chapman explicaba que la inspiración le llegaba en el aislamiento y el retiro de su bañera, o bien mientras garateaba en un trozo de papel de envolver o de papel higiénico, guiada su mano por la musa. De todas formas no fue ningún inventor en el sentido clásico de la palabra; como dijo Peter Warr, Colin tomaba ideas existentes y las perfeccionaba. Y presenció cómo otras personas se fijaban en sus conceptos y los mejoraban, llegando a ganarle con ideas que originariamente habían sido suyas. El Tipo M23, del año 1973, diseñado por Gordon Coppuck, de McLaren, fue la sublimación de una copia robada del Lotus 72. Y a finales de los años setenta los "Wing Cars" de Chapman tipo 78 y 79 inspiraron a Ligier y Williams, sus rivales en la pista, a crear vehículos mucho mejores que el original. De hecho, Chapman era el hombre para el esbozo en el mejor sentido de la palabra: él marcaba el rumbo y delegaba el trabajo fino a sus colaboradores.

El sector lo recuerda por sus repetidos gestos de triunfo y las ovaciones en pie dedicadas a su propia persona. Tras cada éxito de la marca en un Gran Premio, saltaba en la recta final con las piernas abiertas en un paso de ópera y lanzaba su gorra negra al cielo. La última representación tuvo lugar en 1982, cuando en el Circuito Austríaco Elio de Angelis, el bello romano, obtuvo la victoria por muy poco ante Keke Rosberg, el hombre de Williams. Con solo 35, el joven Chapman bromeaba diciendo que se iba a retirar, aunque finalmente fue retrasando la fecha de lustro en lustro. El 16 de diciembre de 1982 un ataque al corazón tomó la decisión por él. En ese tiempo estaba planeando un vehículo con suspensión activa. La muerte de sus conductores, como Mike Spence, Jochen Rindt y Ronnie Peterson le había afectado mucho, especialmente la de Jim Clark en abril de 1968 en Hockenheim, un circuito sin importancia de Fórmula 2.

Chapman el visionario: el progreso siempre tuvo un nombre en la numeración correlativa de sus obras: el registro de un genio de la técnica. El Lotus 25 de 1963 (tan minimalista como bello) se presentó como primer coche de carreras F1 con una estructura de monocasco. La idea que se escondía detrás era unir dos depósitos de gasolina colocados longitudinalmente por medio de un subsuelo portante, dos fuertes mamparas transversales y el cuadro de instrumentos. Los pilotos, especialmente Jim Clark, se colocaban casi tumbados en esta bañera de aluminio. Gracias a este concepto se obtuvieron 14 victorias de Grandes Premios en cuatro temporadas y supuso la primera corona para Clark y el Team Lotus en 1963. Dos años más tarde le siguió los pasos su sucesor directo, el Lotus 33, que cosecharía casi el mismo éxito.

El ejemplar único tipo 38 quedó para la historia como una nota marginal. Fue fabricado con el único objetivo de ganar las 500 millas de Indianápolis en 1965. Victoria relativamente minúscula pero soberana, que consiguió en terreno ajeno con el rápido escocés al volante.

El siguiente hito de Chapman en la historia de la Fórmula 1 fue el Lotus 49 de 1967, que hacía uso de una estructura portante. Este modelo se presentó en el Gran Premio de Holanda en junio de ese mismo año y llevó a Jim Clark a la victoria. A sus espaldas rugía el motor Ford DFV, recién creado por sus padres espirituales, Mike

Costin y Keith Duckworth. Este modelo, un compacto V8 con 32 válvulas, cosechó 155 victorias hasta 1985, y se integraría como elemento de la estructura portadora en el Tipo 49.

Un año más tarde, Chapman se sacó otro as de la manga, esta vez de naturaleza comercial. En el Gran Premio de España en 1968, su vertiginoso parque de vehículos rodó por primera vez en los colores rojo, blanco y dorado de Gold Leaf, su patrocinador. El británico del bigote preparó el golpe en la Fórmula Tasman y en la Fórmula 2, y lo justificó diciendo que en la época de las misiones espaciales, en las carreras de coches también se necesita una técnica ingeniosa. Asimismo, su clase principal se había encarecido mucho desde la introducción de la fórmula de tres litros en 1966. Por ello era necesario buscar fuentes externas de financiación, como por ejemplo un fabricante de cigarrillos, método que se ha mantenido hasta nuestros días.

Gracias al tipo 49 se obtuvieron once victorias, la última en 1970 en Mónaco con Jochen Rindt, donde el veterano Jack Brabham terminó, en la última curva de la última vuelta, en las balas de paja debido a los ataques desenfrenados del ganador. De hecho, en esos momentos el tipo 72 ya era actual, otra revolucionaria creación de Lotus, aun cuando tuvo muchas dificultades iniciales. El 72 resultó ser el monoplaza de la marca con el uso más prolongado ocupando puestos de cabeza en la clasificación. Vestido en los colores negro y dorado de su patrocinador John Player, y conducido por pilotos de la talla de Jochen Rindt, Emerson Fittipaldi o Ronnie Peterson, este monoplaza acumuló entre 1972 y 1975 20 Grandes Premios, tres Campeonatos de Constructores y dos Campeonatos de Pilotos, obtenidos por los pilotos austríaco y brasileño. Las victorias hubieran sido más si Fittipaldi y Peterson, ambos pilotos del equipo, no se hubieran quitado puntos recíprocamente en 1973. Lotus se había mantenido fiel al motor Ford DFV, que se vendió desde 1968 a la mayoría de los fabricantes de coches de Fórmula 1. Las innovaciones más importantes en aquel momento se basaban en la eficiencia aerodinámica, que en el modelo 72 se consiguió gracias al morro en forma de pala y a la cabina del piloto en forma de cuña, flanqueada por dos radiadores situados en los laterales.

El tipo 79 dominó el panorama de la Fórmula 1 solo durante una temporada y fue la herramienta perfecta para los dos campeonatos que Lotus y Mario Andretti se apuntaron en 1978. Lo más llamativo de este coche fue que incorporaba "the unfair advantage". Este es el nombre con el que Chapman designada su querida ventaja injusta: un chasis en forma de "Wing Car" que casi lamía el suelo. El modelo 78 del año anterior, utilizado en las primeras cinco carreras del ciclo de grandes premios de 1978, fue el precursor en el desarrollo en esta dirección. El tipo 79 explotó este principio completamente, lo que le llevó a ser el coche de carreras más atractivo de la década. En 1979 el imperio rojo de Ferrari contraatacó, y los Lotus no llegaron a ninguna parte.

El denominador común de los cinco campeones mundiales Clark (1963 y 1965), Hill (1968), Rindt (1970), Fittipaldi (1972) y Andretti (1978) así como de otros grandes de la Fórmula 1 al servicio de Lotus, como Peterson y Senna, fue, básicamente, que conducían la marca Lotus. En otros aspectos, estos hombres no hubieran podido ser más distintos los unos de los otros.

Stirling Moss, que hizo milagros al volante de los Lotus 18 y 18/21 de la escudería privada de Rob Walker. Jim Clark, unido a Chapman de forma casi simbiótica, piloto rapidísimo y reservado a la vez, cargaba con un profundo compromiso para con su procedencia y patria escocesas. Con razón los medios de comunicación le veían como un hombre que no se podía decidir entre la vara de pastor y la cabina de piloto. Graham Hill, el "londinense del bigote", ya era considerado en vida un monumento por sí mismo y llevaba siempre un casco negro con barras blancas, los colores de su club de remo. Hill sufrió un trágico accidente de aviación a finales de noviembre de 1975, justo cuando acababa de retirarse.

Jochen Rindt, austríaco audaz al que llamaban "Rey de la Fórmula 2", que en 1970, tras su accidente mortal en Monza y a pesar de ello, pasó a ser también un soberano de la Fórmula 1, absurdidades de este deporte. Emerson Fittipaldi, joven, resplandeciente talento que, por así decirlo, anunciaba una tradición de campeones brasileños. Ronnie Peterson ("SuperSwede"), el rubio sueco tranquilo y relajado hacia fuera pero un verdadero volcán al volante y osado como lo fueran Rindt antes que él y Gilles Villeneuve después. Mario Andretti, americano a ratos jovial y a ratos arisco, cuyo legendario carácter polifacético fue lo único que le impidió obtener muchas más victorias en los Grandes Premios. O el gran Ayrton Senna, que se regaló a sí mismo y a la marca Lotus al principio una gran carrera de superlativos con seis de un total de 41 victorias de Gran Premio. Las letras del glorioso Team Lotus ya se encontraban en el firmamento.

El beso que despertó al mito de su largo sueño fue el dinámico empresario Tony Fernandes de Kuala Lumpur. Su equipo Lotus Racing lleva el tradicional esquema de colores verde y amarillo, pero se entiende como una sociedad conjunta anglomalasia que opera más allá de las barreras del Global Village. Sus limpísimos corredores, que en la numeración tradicional de Lotus se llaman T127, aparecieron puntualmente al primer entrenamiento en el inicio de la temporada 2010 en un soleado Bahrain. Antes de la carrera, Clive Chapman, el hijo del difunto Colin Chapman, le regaló a Tony Fernandes la emblemática gorra negra de su padre. En la tarjeta que acompañaba el regalo se leía: "For when next needed": para la próxima victoria. En el año de su debut, se consolidó de forma impresionante como mejor en su clase de entre los nuevos de la fórmula 1. Para 2011 los planes son mucho más ambiciosos. La escudería se llamará Team Lotus de nuevo. El círculo se ha cerrado.

總是領先一步：
蓮花及一級方程式大賽

國際汽車聯盟(Fédération Internationale de l'Automobile) 於2009年9月15日宣布蓮花重回一級方程式大賽。

蓮花, 這個聽來特別響亮的名字, 開啟了通往傳奇的大門。自1950年迄今, 這個團隊在F1大賽排名中仍居於第四位, 在491次的參賽中, 獲得了6次車手冠軍和7次構造車商冠軍, 並逐步累積了79次的勝利和107次桿位。連著名的賽車雜誌Motor Sport都被其愛國的熱情感動而將這個團隊命名為「英國的法拉利」。但是當領先的三巨頭, 義大利的法拉利、麥拉倫和威廉斯勤奮不懈地持續累積積分與排名的時候, 蓮花卻在此時進入長達16年的沉睡期。

縱使不希望破壞蓮花傳奇的名聲, 最後的結果還是令人不勝唏噓。財務吃緊的同時, 一向活力充沛的創辦人又在此時辭世。不屈不撓的改革者科林查普曼太早離開人世, 即使蓮花的標誌上仍留著他名字的縮寫ACBC, 但是團隊的經營卻留下了空窗期。查普曼的車隊經理及繼任者彼得沃爾(Peter Warr)於1985至1987年間曾經讓車隊經營短暫復甦, 這要感謝當時已逐漸嶄露頭角的巴西天才少年阿亞頓塞納(Ayrton Senna)。

科林查普曼(1928－1982)創造力豐富、沒有耐心並且易怒, 從來就不是一個好相處的老闆。被稱為「蓮花先生」的他, 就代表了他創作的車輛。他宣稱是從浴缸的不起眼之處, 或是透過廁紙或包裝紙的潦草塗鴉獲得靈感, 他的手是受到謬思女神所指引, 才能設計出那些名留青史的創作。不過, 科林並不是傳統的發明家。而是比較像彼得沃爾所說的, 他抓住已存在的概念, 然後將其潛在的可能性發揮到極限。查普曼在其他人擷取他的設計概念, 重新改造並在他的遊戲中擊敗他時, 只能冷眼旁觀。喬登考帕克(Gordon Coppuck)於1973年設計的麥拉倫M23就是蓮花72型的仿冒進化版。而查普曼的車翼車款(Wing Cars) 78和79型則是啟發了1970年代賽車場上的競爭對手尼基爾(Ligier)和威廉斯, 讓他們設計出明顯比原創設計還要更好的車子。查普曼是個很有說服力的人, 他的行事風格就是反覆研究一個創作概念, 將其導引到正確的方向 －－然後將細節上的工作丟給他的員工。

賽車界永遠記得當他為自己起立鼓掌時的勝利身影。在他的車隊獲得每一場F1勝利時, 他會在最後一圈賽道上安排一場戲劇演出, 然後將他的黑色帽子拋向空中。他的最後一場客串演出是1982年在奧地利賽道(Osterreichring), 當時帥氣的羅馬車手里利歐. 迪. 安格列(Elio de Angelis)以些微之差從威廉斯的車手柯克羅斯伯格(Keke Rosberg)手中搶下勝利。查普曼總會開玩笑說他要在35歲時退休, 然後再每隔五年延後他自己指定的退休年齡。1982年12月16日突如其來的心臟病發, 讓他從何時退休這個困難決定中徹底解脫。他是在設計一輛主動式懸吊系統的車子時, 被病魔擊倒。麥克史賓塞(Mike Spence)、喬臣林特(Jochen Rindt)和羅尼彼得森(Ronnie Peterson)等車手的辭世已造成他不少損失, 而這些都比不上吉姆克拉克(Jim Clark)於1968年4月, 在霍根海姆(Hockenheim)一場不重要的二級方程式中喪命的損失要來得嚴重。

查普曼的思考方式極具前瞻性, 每一部他所創造的車子都是以連續的號碼來命名, 所有人都可以輕鬆判斷每一車款出現的先後順序。於1963年推出, 如同抽象藝術作品般美麗的蓮花25型, 是第一台以單體結構加入競賽的F1賽車。這款車型的設計是以連接兩個油箱的底盤為基礎, 縱向安裝兩個堅固的橫向車架和儀表板。駕駛的車手吉姆克拉克幾乎是躺在這個鋁製的車體裡。這個概念在4個賽季內贏得了14場F1大賽勝利, 以及1963年克拉克和蓮花車隊的首座冠軍獎盃。兩年後, 這台車的下一代 蓮花33型 也同樣成功。,

蓮花38型則是為了贏得1965年印地安納波里斯500大賽(Indianapolis 500)而特別設計的。這款車型尺寸相對迷你但是容易掌控, 在蘇格蘭車手的操控下, 成功在外國土地上達成它的使命。

下一個讓查普曼在一級方程式的歷史地位更加穩固的里程碑是1967年蓮花49型的問世, 它在當年6月的荷蘭F1大賽中初次亮相。在優勝者吉姆克拉克座位底下發出呼嘯聲響的是一具福特DFV引擎, 這是剛由他的精神之父麥克考斯汀(Mike Costin) 和凱斯達克沃斯(Keith Duckworth)共同研發完成的。這個小型的32氣門V8引擎自推出後直到1985年, 一共獲得了驚人的155場勝利。這個引擎也早已和49型賽車成為一體, 成為承重結構的一個重要元素。

查普曼在次年打出另一張王牌, 這一次的著眼點不在技術, 而是商業上的創新。自1968年的西班牙F1大賽開始, 他的賽車團隊就以漆著其贊助商金樹葉香菸(Gold Leaf)所代表的紅、白、金三色的車體緩緩開向起跑點。這個留著小鬍子的英國人那時也已經為塔斯曼(Tasman)系列賽和二級方程式準備好妙計。他建議在太空時代, 賽車也需要更精密的技術。此外, 3公升方程式的推出, 讓這個賽車的最高殿堂成為更昂貴的活動。因此, 像是香煙製造商等外界資源也開始打入這個市場, 這個現象直到今日仍然存在。

49型賽車創造了11次的勝利, 最後一次是1970年在摩洛哥, 喬臣林特在那裡的猛烈攻勢, 惹惱了傑克布拉漢(Jack Brabham)這個賽車老手, 讓他在最後一圈的最後一個彎道不受控制的離開了賽道, 直衝向一堆稻草。72型賽車是另一個蓮花結構的創舉, 儘管在初期遇到一些小困難, 但仍然緊跟著前輩的腳步。蓮花72型賽車是這個車隊服役最久的露輪車。自1972年起, 在贊助商John Player香煙的黑金色標誌加持下, 加上喬臣林特、艾默森費迪帕爾蒂(Emerson Fittipaldi)和羅尼彼得森這樣的賽車好手, 讓這款車累積了20場的F1勝利、3次構造車商冠軍和奧地利籍及巴西籍兩個車手冠軍獎盃。如果不是費迪帕爾蒂和彼得森在1973年時因為受制於那些難對付的車手而失去積分, 那72型賽車的成績會更驚人。蓮花一直擁護自1968年即賣給主要一級方程式構造商的福特DFV引擎。當時盛行空氣動力學效能的創新方式。72型賽車達成了這個目標, 它配備瘦削車鼻和楔型駕駛艙, 將龐大的散熱器放在車子兩側, 消除了所有空氣動力學上容易引起麻煩的缺陷。

79型賽車為蓮花和馬里奧安德烈提(Mario Andretti)在1978年獲得雙重冠軍, 不過這台完美的車輛卻只主導了一級方程式一個賽季的時間。也許這就是查普曼最愛的「不公平的優勢」的最有力證明。他將這台幾乎緊貼地面的賽車底盤稱為車翼車款(Wing Car), 將F1帶入加裝車翼的時代。前一年亮相的78型賽車也參加了1978年的前5場F1賽事, 踏出往這個方向前進的第一步。79型則將這套原理發展到極限, 也許已成為當時最引人注目的賽車。不過, 法拉利紅色帝國在1979年展開反擊, 而蓮花立刻被遠遠拋在後頭。

五位世界冠軍克拉克 (1963及1965)、希爾 (1968)、林特(1970)、費迪帕爾蒂(1972)和安德烈提(1978), 以及其他曾經身為蓮花車隊一員的F1偉大車手, 例如彼得森和塞納, 都能追溯到他們曾為蓮花車隊出賽的紀錄。的確, 他們都是完全不同的個體。首先是名字幾乎離不開查普曼的吉姆克拉克(Jim Clark), 車速異常快速卻又特別害羞, 是個早已將自己奉獻給家鄉的蘇格蘭人。媒體總是形容他在駕駛座和牧羊人的曲柄仗之間不知該如何抉擇, 這樣的描述的確與事實相差不遠。還有「倫敦大鬍子」葛拉漢希爾(Graham Hill)。他的一生都是傳奇, 他在剛決定退休, 高掛他那有著跟他的划船俱樂部相同顏色, 帶有白色條紋的黑色安全帽時, 竟在1975年11月底於一場墜機意外中喪生。

總是神氣活現的奧地利車手喬臣林特(Jochen Rindt), 被大家稱為「二級方程式之王」, 也是1970年的F1冠軍 – 他是在蒙扎(Monza)撞車死亡後才獲得此頭銜, 這也是這項運動發生過最荒誕的事之一。還有年輕又天賦異稟的車手艾默森費迪帕爾蒂(Emerson Fittipaldi), 他是巴西籍冠軍的先驅。總是一下子平易近人, 一下子又粗魯無禮的美國車手馬里奧安德烈提(Mario Andretti), 如果不是因為他自己傳奇般的多變人生, 也許早就在F1大賽獲得更多成就。金髮的瑞典車手羅尼彼得森(Ronnie Peterson), 在他冷酷又平靜的外表下, 這個「超級瑞典人」其實是個性情猛烈、勇於冒險的車手, 就像他的前輩林特或是後起之秀吉耶維倫紐夫(Gilles Villeneuve)一樣。當然還有偉大的阿亞頓塞納, 他在為蓮花車隊出賽時拿到了他生涯41次F1大賽勝利中的6次勝利, 這也是他職業生涯的巔峰。蓮花車隊的標誌在此時也已經於歷史上留下不容抹滅的地位。

讓蓮花傳奇重生的關鍵人物是來自吉隆坡的企業家東尼費南達斯(Tony Fernandes)。他的蓮花賽車(Lotus Racing)車身漆著和查普曼的蓮花車隊相同的綠色和黃色, 不但是歷史的傳承, 也可以被視為是跨越文化差異的英國及馬來西亞跨國合作案。他那些以蓮花慣用的數字編號命名的閃亮賽車T127系列, 準時在2010年賽季的第一次練習賽中於陽光普照的巴林現身。賽前, 已故的科林查普曼之子, 克里夫查普曼, 特別將其父親的黑色帽子致贈予費南達斯。這個動作隱含的意義為「在你下次需要時可以派上用場」-- 也就是為迎接下次勝利而準備。這個團隊初登場就在F1所有的新成員中展露其令人印象深刻的優勢。在湯尼的帶領之下, 相信這個再次掛上傳奇蓮花車隊標誌的團隊將會在2011年掀起F1賽事的高潮。
 蓮花傳奇又回來了!

TOUJOURS UNE LONGUEUR D'AVANCE: LOTUS ET LA FORMULE 1

L e 15 septembre 2009 la FIA (Fédération Internationale de l'Automobile) a annoncé le retour de l'équipe Lotus en Formule 1.

Les deux syllabes qui conjuguent de façon particulière l'harmonie et l'insolité font ressusciter le mythe. Encore aujourd'hui la marque figure dans la liste des gagnants du Grand Prix suivie depuis 1950 à la quatrième place ayant décroché six fois le titre « meilleur pilote » et sept fois le titre « meilleur constructeur » et emportant 79 victoires et 107 départs en pole position sur un total de 491 courses. Récemment, elle fut surnommée par un journal spécialisé prestigieux et patriotique *Motor Sport*, la « Ferrari anglaise ». Tandis que les trois leaders Ferrari, McLaren et Williams croisent toujours le fer sur la piste en vue de positions et de points sur le chemin de l'immortalité, Lotus tomba dans un profond sommeil durant 16 ans.

Nonobstant la triste fin, l'événement ne put nuire à la légende Lotus. Le manque de moyens financiers et l'absence du fondateur dynamique, à la fois moteur et innovateur sans répit, dont les initiales ACBC (Anthony Colin Bruce Chapman) forment l'emblème de Lotus, en étaient les causes principales. Après la mort prématurée de Chapman, Lotus connut une courte apogée entre 1985 et 1987 sous la direction de son successeur Peter Warr, mais surtout grâce au jeune pilote miracle brésilien plein d'avenir, Ayrton Senna.

Colin Chapman (né en 1928 et décédé en 1982): génial, impatient, rageur, bref, un patron difficile. Ses produits et sa personne devinrent inséparables et on l'appelait « Monsieur Lotus ». Son inspiration, d'après sa propre explication, puisait sur les instants d'isolement dans sa salle de bains où il faisait ses croquis sur un morceau de papier hygiénique ou d'emballage alors que la muse guidait sa main. Toutefois il n'était pas un inventeur au sens propre du terme : « Colin », ainsi Peter Warr, « partait d'idées existantes et les perfectionnait. En revanche, Chapman vivait

l'expérience que les autres adoptèrent ses conceptions, les améliorèrent et finalement emportèrent la victoire grâce à ses idées. » Ainsi le modèle M23 conçu en 1973 par le designer de McLaren Gordon Coppuck était tout simplement une copie sublimée de la Lotus 72. Les « Wing Cars » modèle 78 et 79 de Chapman inspirèrent à la fin des années 70 à ses concurrents de piste, Ligier et Williams, des techniques nettement supérieures à celles d'origine. Enfin, Chapman était plutôt l'homme définissant l'encadrement – il indiqua les grandes lignes aux collaborateurs qui se chargèrent ensuite des détails.

La branche se rappelle de son attitude triomphante répétée et son auto-acclamation. Chaque fois que le GP fut remporté par la marque il sauta jambes écartées, non sans aires dramatiques, sur la dernière ligne droite jetant sa casquette noire en l'air. La dernière fois, lorsque le pilote romain Elio de Angelis remporte sur le Österreichring la victoire, à l'issue d'un sprint final resté fameux pour son faible écart avec le pilote de Williams Keke Rosberg. Le jeune Chapman blaguait et affirma qu'il allait prendre sa retraite à l'âge de 35 ans. Ensuite, aussitôt arrivé le moment, il renvoya sa retraite personnelle sur des étapes de cinq ans. Le 16 décembre 1982, un infarctus pris de façon définitive la décision à sa place, Alors qu'il était en train d'étudier un véhicule avec suspension active. Le décès des pilotes Mike Spence, Jochen Rindt et Ronnie Peterson pesaient lourds dans son esprit, surtout la disparition de Jim Clark dans une course de Formule 2 moins importante en avril 1968 sur le circuit d'Hockenheim.

Chapman le précurseur : Le progrès portait toujours un nom au sein de la numérotation continue de ses œuvres – un répertoire complet des œuvres d'un génie technique. La Lotus 25 de 1963, première monocoque de l'histoire utilisée sur un bolide de Formule 1, à la fois minimaliste et esthétique. L'idée au fond : relier au tableau de bord un châssis composé de deux longerons solides formant deux réservoirs d'essence, soudés sur un plancher métallique. Le pilote, le premier étant Jim Clark, conduisait en position couchée dans cette véritable baignoire d'aluminium. Le concept reporta 14 Grands Prix sur quatre saisons et tressa les premières couronnes de laurier pour Clark et le « Team Lotus » en 1963. Deux ans plus tard, suivait la Lotus 33, un modèle amélioré, couronné d'autant de succès.

Modèle unique resta son héritière, la Lotus 38, étudiée et construite en ayant un seul objectif : gagner les 500 Miles d'Indianapolis. Plutôt de petites dimensions par rapport aux autres bolides, mais souveraine sur le terrain étranger, elle est victorieuse aux mains du pilote écossais.

Avec la Lotus 49 sortie pour la première fois à l'occasion du Grand Prix des Pays-Bas, Chapman marca un autre moment phare dans l'histoire de la Formule 1. Un moteur DFV spécifiquement développé pour la F1 par deux motoristes de génie de Ford,

Mike Costin et Keith Duckworth, mugissait dans la nuque du pilote. Le moteur DFV est un V8 compacte à 32 soupapes qui remporta 155 victoires en Grand Prix jusqu'à 1985. Ce moteur étant déjà incorporé dans le modèle 49 comme élément portant.

Un an plus tard, Chapman sortait un autre atout de la manche. Cette fois-ci il était de nature commerciale. A partir du Grand Prix d'Espagne en 1968 l'écurie apparut dans une nouvelle livrée rouge, blanche et or du sponsor Gold Leaf. Un coup soigneusement préparé par l'anglais moustachu lors de la série Tasman et la Formule 2. A l'époque aérospatiale, ainsi soutenait-il, les sports automobiles exigeaient pareillement l'introduction de la technologie de pointe. En outre, sa classe suprême lui coutait considérablement plus cher depuis l'introduction de la cylindrée de trois litres en 1966. Pourquoi il faut faire recours à des ressources financières extra-sportifs telles qu'un cigarettier – une procédure qui va perdurer jusqu'à nos jours.

Le modèle 49 remportait onze victoires, la dernière en 1970 à Monaco aux mains de Jochen Rindt, qui, avec ses attaques impétueuses contre son adversaire, envoya le pilote expérimenté Jack Brabham au dernier virage dans les bottes de paille. C'était d'ailleurs déjà l'ère du modèle 72, une autre création Lotus pionnière, souffrant initialement de plusieurs défauts de jeunesse. La 72 était la monoposte le plus longtemps en service de la marque leader. Elle remporta à partir de 1972 jusqu'à 1975 avec sa livrée or et noir en raison de son sponsor John Player aux mains des pilotes Jochen Rindt, Emerson Fittipaldi et Ronnie Peterson 20 victoires GP, trois titres de champion du monde des constructeurs et deux titres pilotes pour l'autrichien et le brésilien. Les titres auraient été plus nombreux si les pilotes puissants Fittipaldi et Peterson ne s'avaient pas chipé mutuellement les points précieux en 1973. Lotus restait fidèle au moteur Ford DFV qui était le plus vendu aux constructeurs F1 depuis 1968. L'innovation se concentrant alors plutôt sur l'efficacité aérodynamique. Celle-ci améliora grâce au museau en forme de burin, la carrosserie en coin et les radiateurs latéraux introduits avec le modèle 72.

Pendant toute la saison le modèle 79 s'imposait au monde de la Formule 1. Un outil parfait pour remporter les deux championnats pour Lotus et Mario Andretti en 1978. Ce modèle représentait peut être de façon plus frappante ce que Chapman appela et adora « the unfair advantage » (l'avantage déloyal). L'avantage déloyal consistait dans la forme du châssis à effet de sol des « Wing Cars » permettant d'exploiter l'écoulement de l'air sous la voiture d'où les voitures bénéficiaient d'une tenue de route redoutable. Le modèle 78 qui était sorti l'année précédente et employée pendant les cinq premières courses du cycle GP en 1978 était la première démarche entreprise dans cette direction. Le modèle 79 exploitait ce principe à fond et devint la voiture de course préférée de la décennie. En 1979 s'imposait par contre l'empire Ferrari et marca le début du déclin de Lotus.

Les succès répétés des cinq champions du monde Clark (1963 et 1965), Hill (1968), Rindt (1970), Fittipaldi (1972) et Andretti (1978) ainsi que d'autres grands seigneurs de la F1 et pilotes de la marque tel que Peterson et Senna avaient une chose en commun : ils pilotaient surtout des Lotus. Pourtant les pilotes se distinguaient considérablement l'un de l'autre. Sans oublier Stirling Moss, pilote de la Lotus 18 et 18/21 bleu-blanc du propriétaire de l'écurie Rob Walker, réalisant de vrais miracles. D'abord Jim Clark, presque en symbiose parfaite avec Chapman, pilotant au-delà du rapide, grand timide, écossais et profondément attaché à sa patrie. Les medias le voyaient écartelé entre la houlette et le volant. Peut être il y avait quelque chose de vrai dedans. Ensuite il y avait le « Londonien moustachu » Graham Hill, entré dans la légende de son vivant jusqu'à sa mort tragique dans un accident d'avion, le 30 novembre 1975. Il venait juste de raccrocher son casque noir et blanc (les couleurs de son club nautique).

Puis il y avait l'autrichien farouche Jochen Rindt, surnommé le « Roi de la formule 2 », s'avérant maître de la Formule 1, même après le crash à Monza qui lui coûta la vie – une des absurdités rencontrées dans ce sport. Sans oublier le jeune et brillant talent Emerson Fittipaldi, qui sonna le commencement d'une tradition formelle de champions brésiliens. Le suédois blond Ronnie Peterson surnommé le « SuperSwede », vu de l'extérieur, une personnalité calme et sereine mais éclatant de brio au volant, un pilote « casse-cou » comme l'était avant lui Rindt et après lui Gilles Villeneuve. L'américain « bourru jovial » Mario Andretti souffrant d'une versatilité légendaire qui lui barra la route à de plus nombreuses victoires GP. Et finalement Ayrton Senna qui faisait au début de sa carrière des superlatives, cadeau à lui-même et la marque Lotus en remportant six de ses 41 victoires GP. Alors que le Team Lotus glorieux avait déjà inscrit son nom au palmarès.

La résurrection du mythe est due à l'entrepreneur dynamique Tony Fernandes de Kuala Lumpur. Son écurie Lotus Racing porte la livrée traditionnelle vert et jaune et se considère une joint-venture anglo-malais au-delà des clôtures du *Global Village (village mondial)*. Les bolides brillants appelés T127 en continuant la veille tradition de dénomination Lotus se présentaient à l'heure précise à la réunion des entraîneurs au début de la saison 2010 au Bahreïn ensoleillé. Avant la course, Clive Chapman, fils du Colin Chapman décédé, faisait cadeau de la fameuse casquette noire de son père. Sur le bout de papier accompagnant la casquette était écrit « For when next needed » lui demandant de la jeter en l'air à la première victoire de l'écurie. Dans l'année de son début, l'écurie a su s'imposer parmi les nouveaux venus dans le Championnat F1 comme meilleur de sa classe. En attendant à faire mieux, on a donc fixé la barre plus haute pour 2011. L'écurie portera de nouveau le nom Team Lotus. La boucle sera ainsi bouclée.

CD1
TEAM LOTUS IN FORMULA 1

THE BEST OF THE TEAM LOTUS PODCASTS – 2010 HIGHLIGHTS

1. **THE LOTUS RACING LAUNCH – 29:08**
Recorded at the Royal Horticultural Halls in London this is the original introduction to the team at the launch event in February 2010. Drivers Jarno Trulli and Heikki Kovalainen, Chief Technical Officer Mike Gascoyne and Team Principal Tony Fernandes discuss the first five months of the team's life and what it means to them to see the classic green and yellow livery unveiled for the first time.

2. **MALAYSIAN GRAND PRIX – 38:05**
Recorded before the Malaysian Grand Prix, the team look ahead to their Malaysian home race at the Sepang Circuit. Jarno and Heikki talked through how to drive the the best lap of the challenging Malaysian track and how the drivers deal with the hot and humid conditions. Lotus Racing's third driver Fairuz Fauzy talks about competing in front of his home crowd and Chief Technical Officer Mike Gascoyne looks back at the first two races of the year, the Bahrain and Australian Grand Prix.

3. **MONACO GRAND PRIX – 30:41**
The team preview the jewel in the crown of Formula One™, the Monaco Grand Prix. Jarno Trulli is a previous race winner in the Principality and discusses how to master the tight street circuit while Heikki Kovalainen looks ahead to racing a Lotus F1™ car at one of its spiritual homes for the first time. Team Manager Graham Watson gives an insight into the logistical challenges of setting up the garages and hospitality units and going racing within the incredibly tight confines of Monaco, while Mike Gascoyne and Tony Fernandes look back at the Malaysian and Chines races and the steps forward the team took at the Barcelona Grand Prix.

Team Principal Tony Fernandes and Mike Gascoyne discuss how they first met exactly one year before at the British Grand Prix and drivers Jarno Trulli and Heikki Kovalainen discuss the changes made to the track and their thoughts on racing Lotus F1 cars on home turf in the UK.

6. **HUNGARIAN AND BELGIAN GRAND PRIX – 31:13**
Taking you into the heart of the team, Heikki and Jarno's Race Engineers Juan Pablo Ramirez and Gianluca Pisanello talk about their careers, their relationship with their respective drivers and the role a Race Engineers plays in F1™. Heikki and Jarno give their thoughts on the preceeding European races and Mike Gascoyne gives some insight into the plans for 2011.

7. **ABU DHABI GRAND PRIX – 23:54**
Ahead of the final race of the 2010 Formula One™ World Championship in Abu Dhabi Jarno and Heikki look ahead to the race itself and the team's second season in 2011. Mike Gascoyne talks through the big steps the team is making in preparation for the 2011 season and Chief Executive Officer Riad Asmat gives an overview of the 2010 season.

8. **SEASON REVIEW – 34:32**
The final view inside the team in 2010 sees Tony Fernandes and fellow shareholders Kamarudin Meranun and SM Nasarudin look back on their first season in Formula One™, Heikki and Jarno on their highs and lows this year and giving an inside view on what F1 drivers get up to in the winter break. Wrapping it up is Chief Technical Officer Mike Gascoyne who gives a technical insight on the 2011 car at a critical stage of its development.

CD2
TEAM LOTUS IN FORMULA 1

TEAM LOTUS IMAGES & DOCUMENTARY

Exclusive Team Lotus photographs including behind the scenes-material – plus pictures in high resolution –

0. **THE EARLY DAYS**
1. **PRE-SEASON**
2. **BAHRAIN, MARCH 2010**
3. **AUSTRALIA, MARCH 2010**
4. **MALAYSIA, APRIL 2010**
5. **CHINA, APRIL 2010**
6. **SPAIN, MAY 2010**
7. **MONACO, MAY 2010**
8. **TURKEY, MAY 2010**
9. **CANADA, JUNE 2010**
10. **SPAIN, JUNE 2010**
11. **UNITED KINGDOM, JULY 2010**
12. **GERMANY, JULY 2010**
13. **HUNGARY, AUGUST 2010**
14. **BELGIUM, AUGUST 2010**
15. **ITALY, SEPTEMBER 2010**
16. **SINGAPORE, SEPTEMBER 2010**
17. **JAPAN, OCTOBER 2010**
18. **KOREA, OCTOBER 2010**
19. **BRAZIL, NOVEMBER 2010**
20. **ABU DHABI, NOVEMBER 2010**

BIBLIO-GRAPHY

JOHN BLUNSDEN AND ALAN BRINTON
Motor Racing Year (1961–1976),
Knightsbridge Group of Publications Ltd,
London 1961-1976

JOHN BLUNSDEN
The Power to Win
Motor Racing Publications Ltd,
London 1983

JIM CLARK
Jim Clark at the Wheel
Arthur Barker Ltd, London 1964

PETER DARLEY
Jim Clark, Life at Team Lotus
Coterie Press Ltd, Luton 2007

JACQUES DESCHENAUX
Grand Prix Guide 1950–2009
Charles Stewart & Company, London 2010

BARRY GILL
*John Player Motor Racing Yearbook
(1972–1976)*
The Queen Anne Press, London 1972–1976

BRUCE GRANT-BRAHAM
Lotus, A Formula One Team History
The Crowood Press, Ramsbury,
Marlborough 1994

PETER HIGHAM
The International Motor Racing Guide
David Bull Publishing, Phoenix 2003

CHRISTOPHER HILTON
Conquest of Formula 1
Patrick Stephens Ltd, Wellingborough 1989

DAVID HODGES
A-Z of Grand Prix Cars
The Crowood Press, Ramsbury,
Marlborough 2001

SAL INCANDELA
*The Anatomy & Development of the
Grand Prix Racing Car from 1975*
Haynes Publishing, Sparkford, Yeovil 1990

INNES IRELAND
All Arms and Elbows
Transport Bookman Publications,
London 1994

MIKE LAWRENCE
Colin Chapman, Wayward Genius
The Breedon Books Publishing Company,
Derby 2002

KARL LUDVIGSEN
Colin Chapman, Inside the Innovator
Haynes Publishing, Sparkford, Yeovil 2010

STIRLING MOSS
A Turn at The Wheel
William Kimber and Co. Ltd, London 1961

DOUG NYE
*Theme Lotus, 1956-1986, from Chapman
to Ducarouge*
Motor Racing Publications Ltd,
Croydon 1986

ANTHONY PRITCHARD
Lotus, The Competition Cars
Haynes Publishing, Sparkford, Yeovil 2006

STEVEN SMALL
Grand Prix Who's Who
Travel Publishing Ltd, Aldermaston,
Reading 2000

JOHNNY TIPLER
Ayrton Senna, The Team Lotus Years
Coterie Press Ltd, Luton 2005

MARK WHITELOCK
1½-litre Grand Prix Racing 1961–1965
Veloce Publishing Ltd, Dorchester 2006

Autosport

Motor Sport Digital Archive Collection
(since 1960)